REASON 3

The Complete Course

Robert Innocent

Printed in the United States of America.

info@mimosabooks.com

ISBN 0973735201

Edited by Larry Haise

For Chico, the greatest gift ever given.

Acknowledgments

For those that don't know, creating a book is a lot like climbing a mountain... without a ton of support, there's no way it can be accomplished. Let me first thank the folks at Propellerhead for creating such an amazing music creation tool. Thanks to Big Business and the rock 'em sock 'em team at Mimosa Books for the opportunity to wrestle this audio gorilla to the ground, on time and with creative flair. Thanks to Disco Dan for the use of his keyboard... karaoke night will never be the same. Much love to Mom and Dad, the brothers, Kayroscar and Mini-E (and the whole familia) for your endless support, love and all flair for all things dramatic. A special thank you to Kitty, Tater and the Quad Starrs for your sweetness and love. Ya'll keep me humble and make me a better man each and every day. Finally, deepest thanks to Chico, who spent his last, valiant days next to me as I wrote this book. Your faithfulness and devotion will be with me always.

About the Author

As a child Robert used a pencil to conduct the orchestra playing from his parents' turntable, hoping one day to be Maestro of the Philharmonic. Well, things didn't really end up that way. Now, the only one who calls him maestro is the maitre d' at his favorite restaurant. This didn't quash his lifelong passion for music and all things audio. Combined with his love for technology, he focuses on writing about digital audio and imaging. He lives in Canada.

Introduction

Congratulations and welcome to *Reason 3.0: The Complete Course*, a place where beginners and more seasoned audio enthusiasts can get a thorough understanding of this amazing suite of musical tools.

Making music electronically has changed in leaps and bounds over the past 20 years. The 1980s started a monumental shift that moved away from physical audio equipment (samplers, drum machines, sequencers and so on) to "virtual" devices that could be programmed using a computer – which leads us all the way up to the third incarnation of Reason, the ultimate electronic music creation tool!

Simply put, Reason 3.0 is a complete software package that allows you to make your own songs. You can work solely within the software or integrate with other programs and even external hardware devices. Reason 3.0 includes synthesizers, drum machines, effects and pattern generating devices (and much more) as well as a sequencer for putting it all together into a cohesive song. Top this all off with a massive and comprehensive library of sounds, samples and patches, and you have all you need to create your masterpiece. When you're all done composing, you can distribute your song to be shared or collaborated on with other Reason users. Finally, you can save your song to multiple standard audio formats for all your fans to enjoy.

This book strives to cover almost every tool and device offered in the software. You bring the creativity and, we'll show you how things work. We start off with baby steps: straightforward, easy-to-understand explanations of the different parts of the package. We go over the little details of the devices as well… every button, every switch, every dial. The more you learn, the further you'll go. Along the way, we'll offer you essential nuggets of audio theory to help guide you through understanding how the devices work. We'll give you many pointers, tips and tricks as well. You'll also come across step-by-step instructions that illustrate the practical applications of the different devices.

So good luck and congratulations on purchasing *Reason 3.0 The Complete Course*. You're on your way to learning!

Contents

Chapter 1 Introduction

Chapter 2 The Interface

Chapter 3 The Sequencer

Chapter 4 The Mixer

Chapter 5 Reason Synthesizers

Chapter 6 Device Central

Chapter 7 Effects Devices

Chapter 8 The Combinator and Outputting

Introduction 1

Welcome to the *Reason 3.0 The Complete Course*. Many things may have led you here… a love of music, an interest in technology, the desire to compose, or maybe all of these and more. In the upcoming pages you'll be introduced to one of the most powerful music creation software packages that exits, Propellerhead Software's Reason 3.0. No matter what your level of experience, you'll be able to benefit from this book's logical style of presentation… lots of practical, useful facts and more importantly, step-by-step instructions on how manipulate Reason 3.0 to build an electronic sound that is uniquely yours. The bottom line is simple: Your ability to compose is limitless. The only thing holding you back is your creativity and imagination! This book will be equally informative for both the Mac and PC user… we don't discriminate here, we just demand a curiosity (and maybe even passion) for making music! Here's some subjects we'll discuss in this chapter:

- **What's New in Reason 3.0**

- **How to Launch Reason**

- **Configuring the Preferences Before We Begin**

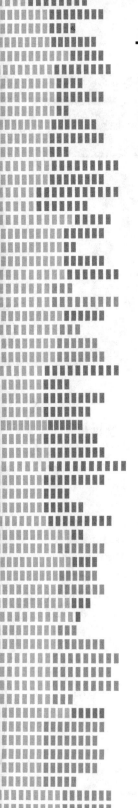

Reason 3.0 is the latest incarnation of this software package and as such offers new tools and toys as well as additions and improvements over previous releases. If some of these advancements don't seem self explanatory at this stage, don't worry, they'll be covered in later chapters.

New Features

- **3.0 Browser** – A powerful database organizer and search engine, this upgraded browser allows you to manage your sounds in an intuitive, easy-to-find way. You can speed your workflow with a free-text search of your entire library and the ability to preview sounds directly from within the browser.

- **3.0 Sound Bank** – A wide array of multi-sampled instruments, sounds and patches that expands upon the previous release's library.

- **Remote** – Simple, plug-and-play integration for a majority of external MIDI devices and hardware control surfaces.

- **The Combinator** – A unique, powerful new device that allows you to combine unlimited Reason devices and chain them together then save them as Combi-patches.

- **Line Mixer 6:2** – A six channel stereo line mixer designed primarily for use with the Combinator.

- **The MClass Mastering Suite** – Combining five devices in one (MClass Equalizer, Stereo Imager, Compressor, MClass Mastering Suite Combi and Maximizer), this tool enhances stereo depth, width and clarity for a professional quality mastered sound.

Upgrades and Improvements

- The ability to record automation onto multiple tracks.

- The ability to copy automation information between different lanes and tracks in the sequencer.

- New and updated muting and soloing features in the sequencer.

- Faster load times of samples.

- Quality and timing improvements for playing back samples.

A Good Reason to Start

Let's begin with the assumption that you have followed the included documentation with Reason 3.0 and it is now installed correctly. It's time to launch the program.

Launching Reason 3.0 on a Mac Running OS X

1. Click on the Go menu.

2. Click on Applications to open the Applications window.

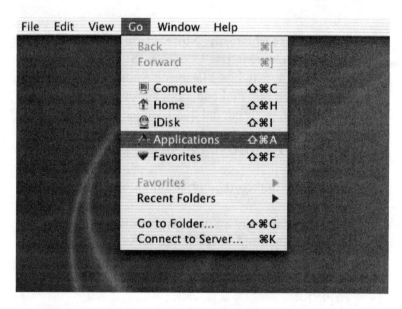

3. Browse to the Reason folder and double click on it.

4. Double click on the Reason program icon. This will launch the program.

Launching Reason 3.0 on a PC with Windows

1. Click on the Start button.

2. Click on All Programs and navigate to > the Propellerhead Group > the Reason Group.

3. Click on the Reason program icon, and the program will now launch.

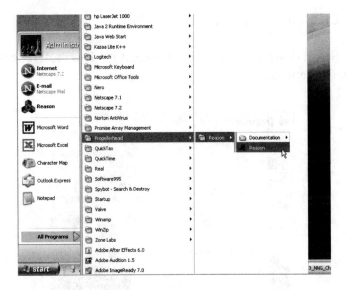

Configuring Reason 3.0

Before we can begin to truly explore the assorted array of goodies that Reason 3.0 has for us, we need to make sure that the preferences are configured properly. To do that, we need to open the Preferences window.

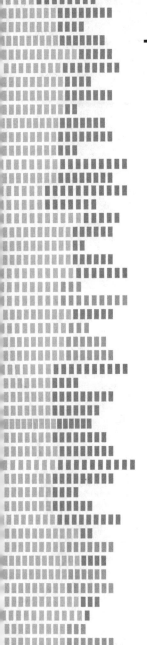

Accessing the Preferences Window on a Mac

1. Click on the Reason menu on the main Reason screen.

2. Scroll down to Preferences to select it.

3. The Preferences window appears.

Accessing the Preferences Window on a PC

1. Click on the Edit menu.

2. Scroll down to Preferences to select it. The Preferences window appears.

The Preferences Window Explained

The Preferences window allows you modify four different preference options that are integral to the operation of Reason 3.0. These are:

- General

- Audio

- Control Surfaces and Keyboards

- Advanced MIDI

They are all accessed by the Page menu. You can select an individual element by either:

- Clicking on the down arrow and selecting the preference option.

- Clicking on the up or down arrows to bring up the unique window for that preference option.

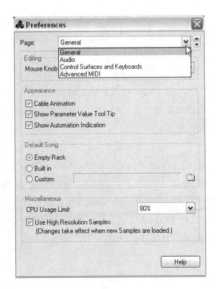

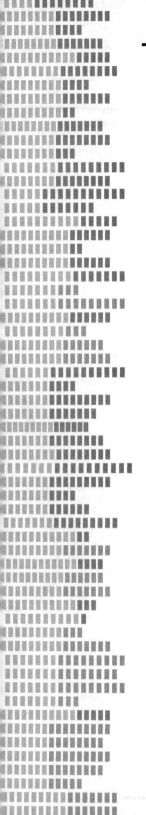

Configuring General Preferences

- **Editing**: **Mouse Knob Range -** This parameter controls the sensitivity of the mouse when adjusting the different knobs within Reason 3.0. There are three options in this pull-down menu: Very Precise, Precise and Normal. The higher precision you select, the more sensitive the knob will be. This means that you will control smaller increments of adjustment with every mouse movement.

- **Appearance: Show Song/ReFill Splashes** - Some users prefer a visual reference for their songs or refill elements when using the browser to organize and access them. If that doesn't appeal to you, deselect this option by removing the check mark from the box and no splash pictures will appear.

- **Appearance: Cable Animation -** Reason 3.0 takes virtual reality a step further by showing you the spaghetti factory of cabling that exists behind a typical real life rack! Too much reality? Uncheck this box!

- **Appearance: Show Parameter Value Tool Tip** - As you are learning how to use Reason 3.0, you might find it useful to find out the name and parameter (or value) of the knob, dial or device that your mouse is currently positioned over. Keep this checked to display that information or uncheck it if you don't want to see it.

- **Appearance: Show Automation Indication -** If you have automated parameters in the sequencer, the buttons and knobs on that device will be outlined by a green box on the related device. If you don't want to see this indicated, uncheck the box.

- **Default Song** - When you start up Reason 3.0, you can select one of three options to appear. **Empty Rack** will start you off in an environment with no devices except the Reason 3.0 hardware interface. **Built in** will select the default song built into the software. **Custom** allows you to browse to and select the song template you wish to start with every time. The benefit here is that you can choose the song you wish to appear when the software is launched .

- **Miscellaneous**: **CPU Usage Limit** - Reason 3.0 is a powerful program that utilizes a great deal of your system's resources. The more you ask from your system to create audio, the less there is for the graphical aspects of it. This limit allows you to dole out amounts of cpu usage specifically for creating audio. The default setting of 80% means that 20% is left for graphics. Tweak this value to get the performance and workflow that is optimum for you.

- **Use High Resolution Samples** - Reason 3.0 can play back samples of many resolutions. Based on the abilities of your sound card, selecting this option means that Reason 3.0 will play back samples in their original resolution. That means 24-bit samples get played back at 24-bit and 16-bit get played back at 16-bit. If this is unchecked, then all samples will be played at 16-bit, regardless of their resolution.

A Bit about Bits and Samples

Since we're toe deep in the world of digital audio now, it's high time introduce two essential terms: sampling rate and bit depth. These terms go a long way in describing the "quality" of our digital audio signal.

Digital audio is basically data (in the form of ones and zeros) representing a sound wave. A sound wave (on its simplest level) is broken down into two parts, Frequency (the "length" of the wave) and Amplitude (the "height" or volume of the wave).

To digitally represent the frequency we "sample" it or break it down at a certain rate, measured over time. CD quality audio is sampled at 44,100 samples per second (44.1 kHz). That means every second of the sound wave is broken down into 44,100 different parts. So if we sampled something at 96 kHz, it would be higher quality because we would be isolating even more of sound wave. More samples mean more faithful reproduction of the sound wave.

Bit depth describes a digital data value (bits) representing the amplitude portion of the sound wave. The higher the number, the greater number of amplitude levels that can be gathered. This means a more accurate representation of the dynamic range of the sound wave. CD-quality audio has a bit depth of 16-bit. Professional quality audio (for composing, mixing, etc.) is usually 24-bit.

Configuring Audio Preferences

By far this is the most critical group of settings to adjust before we begin working hands-on with Reason 3.0. Access Audio Preferences using the Page menu. You can select an individual element by either:

A. Clicking on the down arrow and selecting Audio.

B. Clicking on the up or down arrows bringing up the Audio Preferences window.

- **Master Tune** - You can adjust the global tuning, meaning the tuning of *all* of Reason's sounds and devices, via this slider or the up/down arrow keys. The Master Tune is defaulted to the key of "middle A" at 440 Hz and can be adjusted in increments called cents to a value between -100 and +100.

- **Audio Card Driver** - By far this is the most critical preference to set within Reason 3.0. Clicking on the down arrow will list the audio drivers available for your audio card. In Windows we are looking for the ASIO drivers that will result in the best performance (including lower latency, higher sampling frequencies and support for additional hardware and multiple outputs). The next best choice is the Direct Sound Driver (marked with a DX prefix) followed by MME

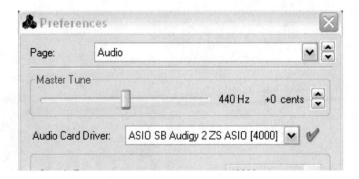

driver. On the Mac side we are ideally looking for the Core Audio drivers for best performance.

- **Sample Rate** - This preference defines the playback sample rate. Note that on some audio driver selections this option will be disabled. If you are using sounds with differing sample rates, they will be re-sampled automatically so that they can be played back. The more different samples you have, the more that will have to be re-sampled, which can affect system performance.

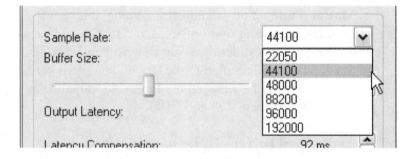

Latency, It's About Time

Or rather, a delay in time. You might also describe it as "reaction" or "response" time. Basically, latency is the duration it takes for audio to go from your application through the workings of the computer and out the speakers. You can also use latency to describe the delay in time from creating input on a MIDI device (such as pressing a note on a keyboard) to hearing it through the speakers. The latency value is determined by your computer audio hardware, audio drivers and settings.

- **Buffer Size and Output Latency -** The output latency
  value is automatically determined by Reason based on
  your computer's hardware/audio card. Depending on
  your driver settings, this option may or may not be
  manipulatible. (For example, this is greyed out when
  you select an ASIO driver.) If you swap to DX or
  MME drivers, you'll notice you can manipulate the
  buffer size slider to affect the number of samples that
  appear. Notice that the greater the number of samples
  you select, the greater the latency time. Ideally, we
  want to have the lowest latency possible, but this may
  affect the quality of the playback. Generally speaking,
  let's try to use the best drivers possible and let the
  computer do the work figuring out these numbers.

- **Latency Compensation -** This value has to do with
  Reason 3.0's synchronization with an external MIDI
  device. If there is a delay issue between the device and
  your computer, you'll want to adjust this value.

- **Active Channels -** This preference will be disabled
  unless you are using ASIO/Core Audio drivers. This
  shows the number of outputs that your hardware
  supports. Most likely the number shown here will be 2
  (for the typical stereo audio card). Some audio cards
  are capable of a great number of outputs (for instance,
  ones that offer surround sound out multiple speakers).
  By clicking the Channels button, you can activate the
  stereo pairs you desire. This will be reflected visually
  in the Reason hardware interface.

- **Clock Source -** Again, this preference is only available on some ASIO/Core Audio driver based cards. Typically, though, this will be greyed out and defaulted to internal. The point of the audio clock is to act as a source to synchronize the sample rate for audio playback. Some audio cards will allow you to synchronize to an external source.

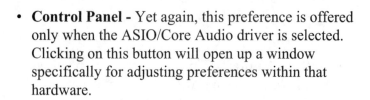

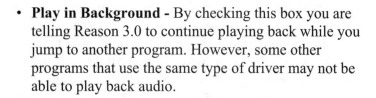

- **Control Panel -** Yet again, this preference is offered only when the ASIO/Core Audio driver is selected. Clicking on this button will open up a window specifically for adjusting preferences within that hardware.

- **Play in Background -** By checking this box you are telling Reason 3.0 to continue playing back while you jump to another program. However, some other programs that use the same type of driver may not be able to play back audio.

Control Surfaces and Keyboard Preferences

This is the area where you configure and set up MIDI devices that you have connected to Reason 3.0.

- **Attached Surfaces** - This list, located in the middle of the preferences box, shows all the devices that have currently been found. By selecting one of the devices you can choose to delete or edit it by clicking on the appropriate button at the bottom.

- **Auto-detect Surfaces** - Selecting this button will initiate a scan for any control surfaces that are connected via a two-way MIDI or USB connection. This will only work with control surfaces that support auto detection.

- **Make a Master Keyboard** - By selecting a MIDI device from the Attached Surfaces list, then clicking this button, you make it the Master (default) Keyboard for MIDI input.

What Exactly is MIDI?

*MIDI is an acronym standing for **M**usical **I**nstrument **D**igital **I**nterface. Very simply, MIDI is a standard (and a fairly old one at that… it's existed since 1983). On the software level it is a protocol that allows electronic musical devices to communicate back and forth in a similar fashion to the way two (or more) computers communicate via a network. On the hardware side it defines the type of connectors that plug into these devices.*

Configuring Advanced MIDI Preferences

In this category we configure Reason to work with external sequencers. This can be done by…

A. Clicking on the down arrow in the Page menu and selecting Advanced MIDI.

B. Clicking on the up or down arrows to bring up the Advanced MIDI Preferences window.

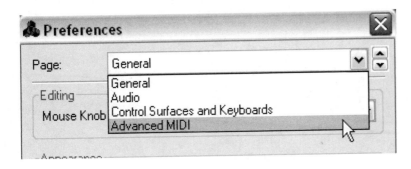

- **External Control** - Here you have the ability to define the MIDI input sources for four buses (A-D) with 16 channels available on each. These devices could be external hardware sequencers or another application running on your computer that acts as a sequencer.

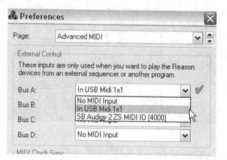

- **MIDI Clock Sync -** With this setting you are defining how you'd like to synchronize Reason 3.0 to external devices.

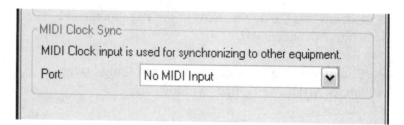

The Interface 2

Aside from the choices that we can select from the pull-down menus, all of the work that we do to create digital music is done via the Reason 3.0 Interface. All of the tools are visually illustrated right in front of us, and we can interact with them as if they were physical devices… we can turn knobs, flip switches, press buttons… even flip the devices over to see the cabling behind them! In Chapter One we took the time to ensure that all the preferences were configured correctly. While that was necessary work to set things up, I'll bet by now you're itching to actually start playing around and dive into Reason 3.0's work space. In this chapter we'll do an overview of the interface and find out the way that things are organized, as well as the most commonly used tools. In a few moments we'll be playing our first song! In this chapter we'll discuss:

- **The Rack**

- **The Reason Hardware Interface**

- **How to Play Your First Reason Song**

- **The Reason Transport Control in Depth**

The User Interface

The Reason 3.0 interface is broken up into three basic regions: The Rack (including the Reason Hardware Interface and Sound Modules), The Reason Sequencer and the Reason Transport.

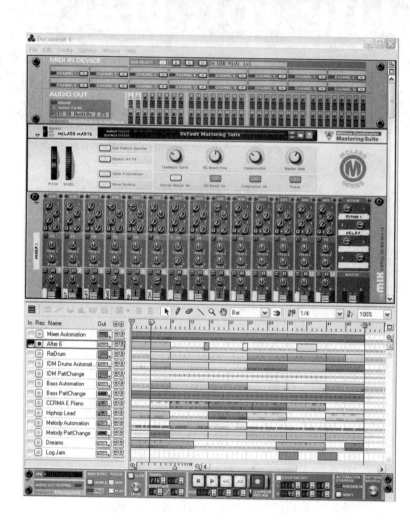

Welcome to the Rack

At the top of very top of the screen just beneath the menu bar
is where Reason 3.0's graphical interface starts. This top
portion is called the Rack. Why the Rack? Well, it has been
designed to replicate (with amazing detail) different real-life
audio components that would be mounted onto an actual rack
in a sound studio. (A rack is basically a metal shell into
which are bolted different devices.) In fact, look at the sides
of the devices and you'll see virtual screws virtually bolting
the devices to the rack mounts! The first device you'll see,
which is located at the very top of the rack, is the Reason
hardware interface. It is divided into two sections: MIDI In
Device and Audio Out. The purpose of the Reason hardware
interface is to act as a junction point between hardware and
the Reason 3.0 software. It's here where we can identify
what hardware is bringing in data (via the MIDI In Device)
and also the hardware destination of data coming out of
Reason 3.0 (Audio Out).

The Reason Hardware Interface

*This feature is an essential part of the software
and will always appear at the top of the rack. It
cannot be moved or deleted.*

MIDI In Device

The first part of the Reason hardware interface we see is the MIDI In device. The purpose of this component is to route incoming MIDI data to different Reason devices. We touched on MIDI routing briefly when we configured the advanced MIDI preferences. We will return to this component in a later chapter when we describe how to add MIDI devices to connect with Reason 3.0.

Audio Out

Here we are defining where we'd like to route the data that leaves the software. In essence, we are identifying the audio signal destination. There are two possibilities: ReWire and Audio Card.

- **ReWire** – This is an advanced feature that allows Reason 3.0 to synchronize and work with a second audio program. For example, you could compose your tracks in Reason and then send them out via ReWire to be mixed (in real time) in another application. To the right you'll see 64 individually numbered channel meters. Here you could monitor the levels of the channels being outputted to another application.

- **Audio Card** – This is tied to the audio preferences we configured earlier. In the lit up green window beneath Audio Card, you'll see indicated the driver for the audio card you selected. Notice that of the 64 individual channel audio meters, the first two are outlined in white with green lights lit beneath the numbers. These are your stereo out channels. If you selected an audio driver that allowed more channels, you'd see these indicated by a green light above the ones that are available.

The Default Audio Out

The default audio out is in the window beneath the lit up green box to the left of the audio card.

There's Much More to the Rack

The rack is where all the tools for making, mixing, effecting and essentially creating your sound are housed. Here you'll be able to find:

- **Mixers** – Reason 3.0's standard 14:2 mixer (called reMIX) and a new mixer, Line Mixer 6:2.

- **Sequencer** – Matrix Analog Pattern Sequencer.

- **Synthesizers** – SubTractor Polyphonic Synthesizer, Malström Graintable Synthesizer.

- **Samplers** – NN19 Digital Sampler, NN-XT Advanced Sampler.

- **Drum and Loop Devices** – Redrum Drum Computer, Dr:Rex Loop Player

- **Effects Generators** – RV-7000 Advanced Reverb, Scream 4 Distortion, BV512 Digital Vocoder, RV-7 Digital Reverb, DDL-1 Digital Delay Line, D-11 Foldback Distortion, ECF-42 Envelope Controlled Filters, CF-101 Chorus/Flanger, PH-90 Phaser, UN-16 Unison, COMP-01 Compressor/Limiter, PEQ-2 Two Band Parametric EQ

- **Utilities & Miscellaneous Tools**– Spider Audio Merger and Splitter Digital Sampler, Spider CV Merger and Splitter, The Combinator, MClass Mastering Suite, ReBirth Input Machine

The greater part of this book will be spent on examining and learning how these different sound modules work and, as well, we'll spend some time explaining how they interconnect and function within the rack. So stay tuned!

Playing Your First Reason Song

In order to play your first song, you must have one loaded! Hopefully, you've got the Reason 3.0 built-in song loaded.

Selecting the Default Song

Remember that under General Preferences we could select the default song. If you didn't select Built in, the song won't be loaded when you start up Reason 3.0.

Playing is very easy. First identify the Reason transport control. It's easy to find at the very bottom of the interface!

1. Find the Play button, which is roughly in the center of the transport control.

2. Click on it once, and the button will turn yellow to show that it's activated.

Now you should be hearing your first Reason 3.0 song! Try pressing the space bar key to stop and then restart the song. You've learned your first keyboard shortcut! No audio? Trying checking these things:

- On the Reason hardware interface check that right Audio Card driver is selected. See Chapter 1, section "Audio Preferences" for information on how to change this.

- Make sure your speakers are turned on!

- If the built-in song wasn't selected in the general settings, go back and make sure it is, then restart Reason 3.0, if necessary.

The Reason Transport Control

Based on what you've just learned, I'm sure you'll surmise that the transport control works just like so many devices that you're familiar with, from a tape deck or cd player to a mp3 or dvd player. It is that, but it's much more as well! Let's take a moment to familiarize ourselves with the different aspects of the Reason transport control.

CPU

This meter shows how much demand Reason 3.0 is placing on your processor. It is specifically showing the demand used by the Reason audio engine and does not include MIDI resources or graphical aspects or other parts of the program. If you're in the green, then you're OK.

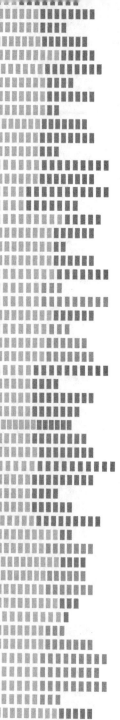

Audio Out Clipping Indicator

The term clipping is used describe a signal overload. What you'd hear is a momentary cutting out of audio. If this indicator lights up, it means the output level is too high for your audio card to handle and needs to be reduced.

MIDI Sync and Focus

Clicking on the Enable button activates MIDI Sync Mode and indicates that you want to switch from Reason 3.0's internal sync clock to receive MIDI sync from an outside source. When Reason is linked to that source, a green light will appear next to Sync Input. The MIDI Focus and Play Focus buttons tell Reason which song(s) have priority (for MIDI data or sync) when there are multiple songs loaded. The MIDI Focus button determines which song has the priority to get MIDI data. The Play Focus button determines which song has priority to get MIDI Sync. If both buttons are lit up, then all MIDI information will be sent to that song, even if it's not currently selected (or in "focus").

Click

An essential element in making any kind of music is keeping in time. Traditionally, this would be done with a metronome, and that's exactly what the Click function is: Reason 3.0's built-in metronome. To activate it, simply press the button next to Click so that it glows yellow. Adjusting the level dial affects the volume of the metronome. This is a great opportunity to learn how to manipulate the value of the dial.

1. Click and hold the mouse button down over the Level dial.

2. A red box will appear with white letters that read "Level" and a numeric value.

3. Still holding down the mouse button, slowly move your cursor up. The value in the Level box will increase, and the animated dial will rotate to the left.

4. Now, while still holding down the mouse button, pull the cursor down. The value decreases, and the animated dial rotates to the left.

Tempo and Signature

The tempo (or speed) of your song is measured in bpm (beats per minute). This is the value indicated by the box on the left side. You can change the values in this box by using the spin controls (the up/down arrow keys immediately to the right of the box). By clicking once you change the value in steps, a single digit at a time. Pressing and holding down either of the arrows will rapidly change the value. You can also change the value the same way that you did with the dial: by pressing and holding your mouse button down over the field and scrolling the mouse up (for a great value) or down (for a lesser value). The box to the right of this one allows you to fine tune the bpm in increments of 1/1000ths.

Numberpad Shortcuts

You can use the keyboard numberpad to change the values in the fields by clicking the (+) plus sign to increase the value or the (-) minus sign to decrease the value.

The Time signature indicates the number of beats per bar (left field) and the length of the bar (right field). These values are changed in the same manner as the tempo values.

The Metronome

Before you have a song composed, you can preview the pace of the tempo and signature activating the metronome in the Click portion of the transport control.

Main Transport Controls

By working with the transport controls we are going to be introduced to a new element of the interface, the Reason sequencer. You'll find the sequencer directly above the transport panel. This is where we put together our musical arrangement to create our song. We will be going deep into the workings of the sequencer in the next chapter. It's safe to say that you're probably an expert when it comes to the first two buttons on the transport controls: stop and play. By now, you even know the keyboard shortcut for playing and stopping... the space bar. The next two keys are very easy to understand too. Let's find out how these keys work in the hands-on way...

1. Press the space bar to start playing the built-in song.

2. While the song is playing, press the Fast Forward button (two arrows pointing right). Notice that it does not play faster but actually jumps ahead to the next bar, then starts playing from there.

3. Press and hold the Fast Forward button for a few seconds. The Position locator (the vertical line that moves through the sequencer, which has a letter P at the top it) advances quickly bar by bar until you stop pressing the Fast Forward button. Once you release the button, it continues playing from the new location.

4. Play the song again and now try the Rewind button. It works in exactly the same fashion, but in this case it's rewinding (or moving to the left).

The Record Button

This red button is used when you have a MIDI keyboard connected to Reason 3.0 and wish to record the notes you perform. There are two different record modes, Overdub and Replace. In Overdub mode, your composition is inserted into the song, starting wherever the position indicator is parked. In Replace mode, the notes you play will overwrite (replacing or deleting) any previous notes. We'll discuss this in great detail when we learn about using the MIDI keyboard.

Transcript Control Shortcuts

As you become more adept at Reason 3.0, you'll want to use keyboard shortcuts instead of moving around. You can use your keyboard's numeric keypad to control the transport functions.

Play – Enter key

Stop – Zero (0) key

Rewind – Seven (7) key

Fast Forward – Eight (8) key

Record – Asterisk (*) key

Go to Left Locator – One (1) key

Go to Right Locator – Two (2) key

Space Bar – Play/Stop

Spend a moment trying these shortcuts. I'll bet you'll find them much more appealing to use than pointing and clicking with your mouse!

Song Position

Underneath the main transport controls are three fields that show us exactly where the position indicator is parked in the sequencer. We can jump anywhere in the song by filling in the values for Bar, Beat and 16th note, respectively.

Loop On/Off

Turning Loop mode on means that when you press Play you will repeatedly hear a region selected in the sequencer. This region is indicated by the left and right locators. They look similar to the Position locator except with the letters "L" for left and "R" for right at the top. You can place them in position in the same manner as you did with the Song Position mentioned above by filling in the Bar, Beat and 16th note values for both left and right locators.

Automation Override

Overriding automation that's on a track or set up on a device with new manual values will cause the "Punched In" indicator to light up. When you press the Reset button, the automation will regain control.

Pattern Shuffle

To create a more rhythmic feel to some of the pattern-based devices in Reason 3.0 (such as ReDrum and Matrix Pattern Sequencer,) you can adjust this knob. Specifically what this does is delay all sixteenth notes between eighth notes. The more you turn this knob to the right, the greater the delay (or shuffle). The effect of slightly changing the timing produces a more naturalistic sound.

The Sequencer 3

In this chapter we will further examine the Reason 3.0 interface, and in particular the most essential part of the program, which is the Reason sequencer. Picking up where we left off in Chapter 2, you'll recall how we used the Reason transport panel to navigate within the sequencer. Let's take some time to find out a little more about its different parts. In this chapter we'll learn:

- **Expanding and Detaching the Sequencer Window**

- **Zooming and Different Views within the Sequencer Window**

- **The Position Indicator and Right and Left Locators**

- **The Sequencer Toolbar in Detail**

What Is a Sequencer?

A sequencer is a device that "plays" a musical composition. Interconnected to other devices that can create sounds (synthesizers, drum machines, samplers, etc.,) it indicates what musical notes to play and when to play them. Imagine it as digital sheet music that can actually control the instruments and tell them what to play.

Introduction to the Reason 3.0 Sequencer

The Reason sequencer is where we compose our musical piece. There are two essential methods to do this: recording via a MIDI device, or working in conjunction with the sound modules to create sounds, patterns, loops, etc. The Reason sequencer sits right above the transport panel. The layout is very straightforward. Horizontally across the top is a palette of tools called the sequencer toolbar. Beneath and to the left is a list of track names, and to the right are the tracks located in the timeline, which is where you build your musical sequence. The time frame encompassed by the sequencer is marked by the Measure ruler (seen at the top, just beneath the toolbar), which is set up in bars with hash marks that break them down into smaller increments.

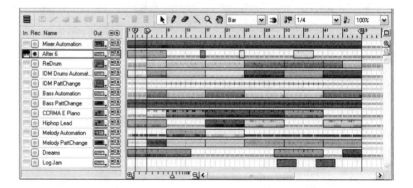

Expanding the Sequencer

Since our attention is now focused on the sequencer, let's expand it in size so that it fills the whole interface.

1. To the far right of the Measure ruler is a Maximize button used to expand the sequencer. Click it once.

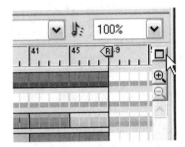

2. The sequencer expands to fill the whole interface, with only the Reason transport visible at the bottom.

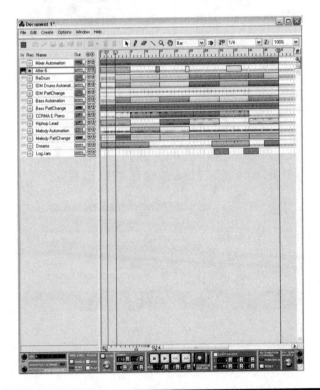

Returning the Sequencer to Its Default Size

Returning the sequencer to its original size is easy.

1. Click on the Maximize/Restore button at the far right of the Measure bar.

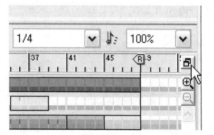

2. The sequencer snaps back to fit in the rack as before.

An Alternate Way to Expand

Another way to expand the sequencer is by positioning your cursor so that it is just above your tools palette and just under the mixer. You'll notice that it changes from a regular arrow type cursor to one that looks like two horizontal lines with an arrow pointing up and an arrow pointing down.

1. When your cursor looks like this, click and hold the mouse button.

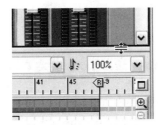

2. Drag upward to the top of the interface.

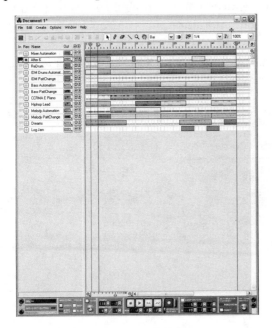

You've now expanded the sequencer to fit the whole screen.

An Alternate Way to Restore

Similar to the alternate way to expanding the sequencer, you position your mouse above the expanded sequencer so that the cursor changes.

1. Click and hold the mouse button.

2. Drag downward revealing the rack elements underneath.

You've now returned the sequencer to its default size.

Detaching the Sequencer

If you'd like to go beyond the limits of the interface and simply have the sequencer fill the whole screen, you can detach it completely. One benefit of doing this is that if you have two monitors you can drag the detached sequencer over to your second monitor to maximize your workspace.

1. Click the Window menu and scroll down to select Detach Sequencer Window.

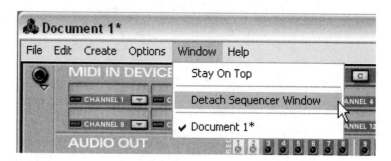

2. With the sequencer window detached you can click on the Maximize button in the upper right corner to have it fill the whole screen.

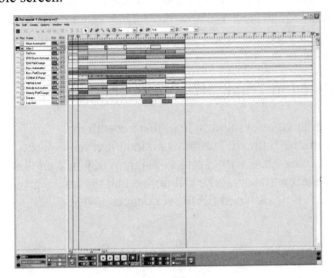

Reattaching the Sequencer Window

Identically to the way you detached the window, simply go to the Windows menu and scroll down to select Attach Sequencer Window. A much easier way is to simply close the window. Finally, clicking on the Maximize/Minimize button will return the sequencer window to its original location.

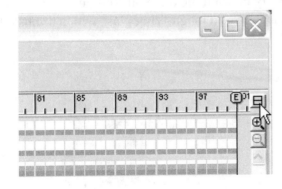

Different Views in the Sequencer

Using what you've just learned, expand the sequencer to fit the whole interface. We now have much more room to work with, but it seems all the tracks are bunched up at the top of the sequencer.

Increasing Track Size (Vertical Zoom In)

At the far right of the timeline, just beneath the Maximize/Minimize button, is an icon that looks like a magnifying glass with a plus (+) sign in it. Click on this button a few times and you'll notice that the tracks grow larger (vertically) and fill the sequencer.

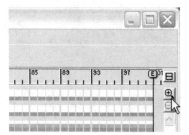

Reducing Track Size (Vertical Zoom Out)

You can make the track size smaller by clicking the icon immediately beneath the one you were just working with. This is the icon of a magnifying glass with a minus (-) sign in it.

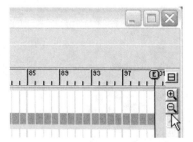

The Vertical Scroll Bar

At the far right of the sequencer window is the vertical scroll bar. You can use the vertical scroll box to navigate through your tracks, particularly when you are zoomed in and the tracks are of large size and when there are more tracks than can be shown in the Sequencer window.

Horizontally Zooming In

At the very bottom left of the sequencer (just above the transport panel) you'll find a zoom bar. It is flanked by a Zoom In icon (plus sign in magnifying glass) to the left and a Zoom Out icon (minus sign in a magnifying glass) on the right. Click a few times on the Zoom In button. As you are doing this, look upwards to the Measure bar. The more you click on this button, the more you zoom into the time and the more time increments will be visible between the bars. The indicator on the zoom bar will move to the left until you are zoomed in the maximum amount.

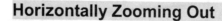

Horizontally Zooming Out

Click a few times on the Zoom Out button. On the Measure bar you'll see a greater amount of time visible while in the timeline you'll see more of your entire song. On the zoom bar the indicator will move to the right until you are zoomed out the maximum amount.

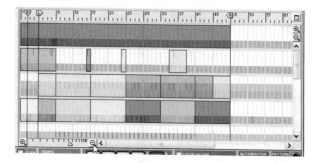

An Alternate Zooming Method

You can quickly zoom in and out horizontally using this method:

1. Click and hold the small house-shaped icon in the zoom bar. It will turn grey.

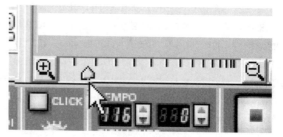

2. Drag the icon to the left to zoom in and to the right to zoom out.

The Horizontal Scroll Bar

Immediately to the right of the zoom bar is the scroll bar. The deeper you are horizontally zoomed into the timeline, the smaller the duration of time of time you are actually viewing. You can see this by looking at the horizontal scroll bar. The Scroll box will be tiny, and by clicking and dragging it you can scroll throughout the duration of your song. As you zoom out more and more the full duration of the song in your timeline will be represented. The scroll box will appear larger and larger until the point when you are zoomed out completely and there will be no scroll box at all.

The Magnify Tool

Let's take a very quick sneak preview of one of the tools in our sequencer toolbar. In the course of creating your song, you will likely want to turn your attention to a particular point in time that happens on a particular track. Using the Magnify tool on the toolbar you can quickly zoom in both vertically and horizontally anywhere within the timeline. The Magnify tool looks like (surprise!) a magnifying glass.

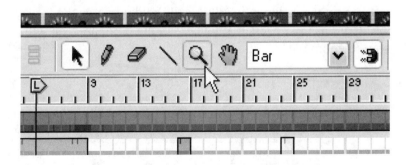

1. Click on the Magnify tool. The icon on the toolbar is depressed.

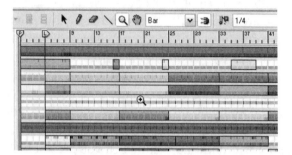

2. Your cursor is now changed to a magnifying glass with a plus (+) sign in it. Click anywhere in the timeline.

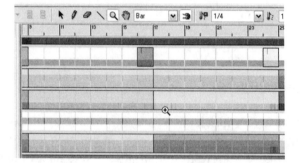

3. Click some more. Wherever you've placed your cursor, you zoom in both horizontally and vertically to that position.

4. Hold down the Ctrl key (Command key on a Mac.) Notice the cursor has now changed to a magnifying glass with a minus (-) sign in it. While still holding down the Ctrl/Command key, click anywhere in the timeline. You will start to zoom out.

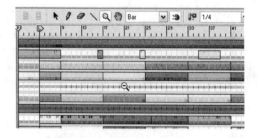

The Sequencer Timeline

The sequencer timeline is composed of two columns. At the left is the Name column and to the right are the sequencer tracks.

The Name Column

The Name column shows in a very easy-to-understand way where MIDI data is coming from and where it is going.

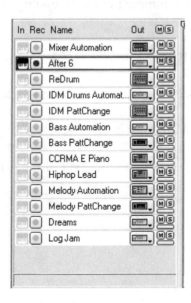

The In Column

The keyboard icon in this column indicates that the track is enabled and therefore ready to receive MIDI data from a connected device such as a keyboard. When you enter data (by hitting keyboard keys) a vertical level meter will light up above the keyboard icon.

The Record Column

The purpose of the red dot icon in this column is to show that the track is ready to record. It's important to note that the record method you have chosen in the Reason transport (overdub or replace) will directly affect the data in that track.

The Out Column

This pull-down menu defines the Reason device where you choose to route the incoming MIDI data.

The Mute Button

Clicking on this will mute the sound on this track during playback.

The Solo Button

Clicking on this will solo this track's playback.

The Level Meter

This will show you the volume level of the playback for this track.

The Position Indicator

In the previous chapter when we discussed the Reason transport, we noticed something happen within the timeline when we played our song. A line with a letter "P" on top of it, which cut vertically across all our tracks, moved in real time from left to right. This is the Position indicator, and as it obviously states, it shows us the location of where we happen to be situated in our song. The Position indicator allows us instantaneous random access anywhere in the timeline.

1. Click anywhere in the Measure bar. The Position indicator automatically jumps to that position.

2. Position your cursor over the top of the Position indicator where the letter "P" is.

3. Click and hold the mouse button down and drag the Position indicator anywhere you want it.

Notice also that if you look to the song position information in the transport bar, you can see numerical values (of bar, beat and 1/16th note) showing where you have placed the Position indicator.

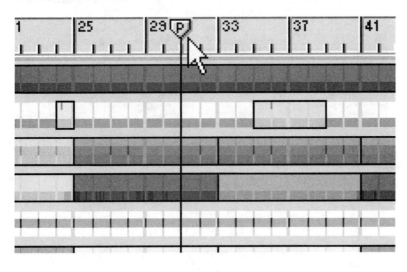

The Left and Right Locators

The left and right locators are used to isolate a region within the timeline that you would like to loop during playback. Don't confuse this with creating loops (we use the Dr:Rex loop player to do that – a maneuver we'll discuss in a later chapter). When you are composing your song, you may want to play a region of it (or all of it) and have it repeat over and over again as you fine tune it. We can identify the area we want to loop by positioning the left and right locators. We can position them in two ways. In the previous chapter we described how we can enter values for left and right locators within the Reason transport. We can also select whether we'd like to turn the looping feature on or off. We can also manually move the locators in the same fashion as we moved the Position indicator.

1. In the measure bar maneuver your pointer over the "L" at the top of the left locator.

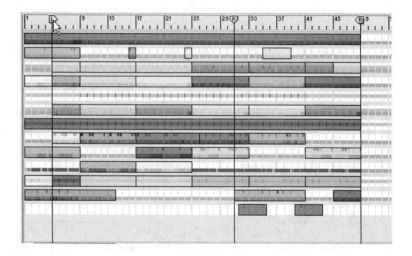

2. Click and hold the mouse button down and drag the left locator to the right.

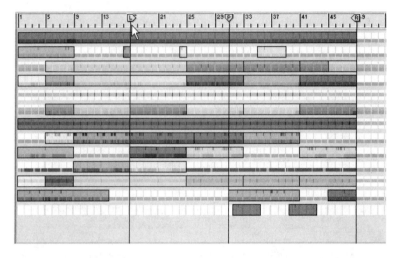

3. Move your pointer over the "R" at the top of the right locator.

4. Click and hold the mouse button down and drag the right locator to the left and position it so that the length of about one bar separates the two locators.

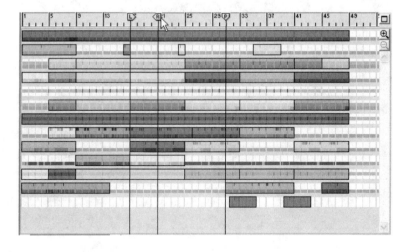

4. Position your cursor over the top of the Position indicator where the letter "P" is.

5. Click and hold the mouse button down and drag the Position indicator to between the locators or to the left of the left locator.

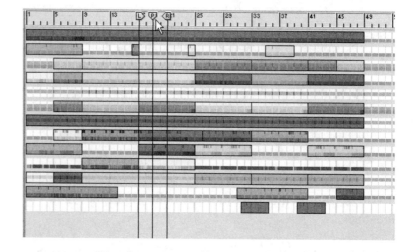

Position Indicator Location

Even if you have Loop On/Off turned on in the Reason transport, if the Position indicator is not between the left and right locators, it will not loop. If it is located before the loop area (meaning to the left of the left locator) and you start to play, when the Position indicator reaches the region bounded by left and right, it will begin to loop once it reaches the right locator. If it is positioned after the loop area (meaning to the right of the right locator), it will not loop at all.

6. Press the Play key in the Reason transport or press the space bar. Reason will play the song between the locators repeatedly.

The Sequencer Toolbar

As described earlier, the sequencer toolbar sits atop the sequencer timeline and track list and has a variety of icons. Let's take a few moments to familiarize ourselves with the different tools available and learn what their functions are.

The Arrange/Edit Mode Button – Part I, Arrange Mode

The first icon you see on the very far left of the toolbar is the Arrange/Edit mode button. This button allows us to toggle between the modes showing how different MIDI data are depicted in the timeline. The default mode is Arrange, whose icon is depicted by three horizontally stacked, colored bars. This mode displays the arrangement of your sequence in the form of ungrouped and grouped MIDI events. MIDI events are the sequencer equivalent of notes on sheet music. A MIDI event contains information about the key the note is to be played in, as well as the velocity, duration and other information.

Typically, the type of editing you'll do in Arrange mode involves using these groups to build the sequence of your song. Also, in this mode you see and can work with all tracks simultaneously.

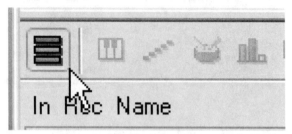

Grouped Events

In the section above, we mentioned that the editing mode you select defines the manner in which you'll view your MIDI data. In Arrange mode you'll notice colored blocks running horizontally along some of the tracks in the timeline. Theses are groups, and they represent a cluster of notes that you feel should be lumped together. (Ungrouped notes are seen as plain white tracks.) You can also tie together multiple groups and even groups spread across multiple tracks. Groups can also be cut, pasted and copied. Why group at all? It helps to organize sounds that are tied together – such as phrases of a song or sounds that you want to repeat. Grouping also allows you to apply identical settings to these bunches of notes. Later we'll discuss how to group and ungroup notes.

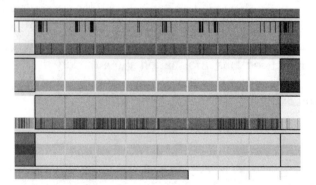

The Arrange/Edit Mode Button – Part II, Edit Mode

Clicking on the Arrange/Edit mode button will toggle to Edit mode, and you can see the icon changes to two white horizontal bars with red and blue blocks within them. Whereas in Arrange mode, where you were editing groups of notes, in Edit mode you tend to edit the individual notes (or events) within a group. In Edit mode you are offered six unique views of the MIDI data. Using these specific views enables you to both create and make changes in the MIDI values (such as note, velocity, pattern, controller information, etc.) in the various tracks. When you select Edit mode, you activate the next six icons, known as the Lane buttons. In this mode you work with one track at a time.

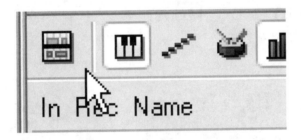

The Lane Buttons

Each Lane button activates a view of specific MIDI data for a single track within the timeline. Certain types of data correspond to certain sound modules. You can display as few as none or as many as all six types of data simultaneously by pressing all of the Lane buttons. Remember, though, that since some Lane data – musical note data for a drum machine, for example – are sound module specific, there may be no data to display if it's irrelevant to that device.

The Key Lane

The first lane icon (which looks like piano keys) is appropriately named the Key lane. When we click on this button, we can see a vertically aligned piano keyboard on the far left of the timeline. This view allows us to see the MIDI data relating to musical notes that are occurring over time. We would use this view when editing data used in such devices as the Malström, NN-19, NN-XT and SubTractor sound modules.

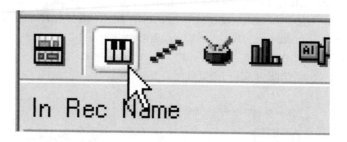

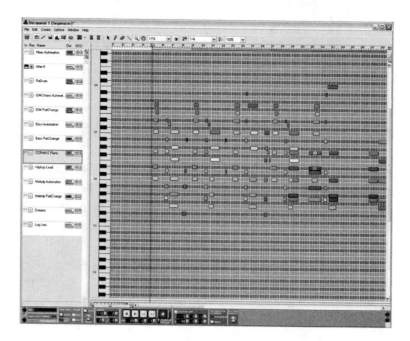

The REX Lane

The second lane icon, resembling diagonal stair steps, is called the REX lane. This lane shows us the MIDI data representing slices (samples of individual beats) and is used when editing within the Dr:Rex loop player.

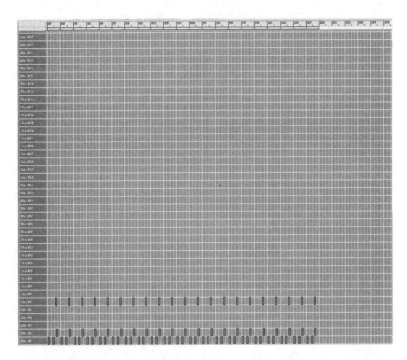

The Drum Lane

The Drum lane is easily identified by the icon of a snare with two drumsticks, and it's with this view that you'd edit MIDI data related to the Redrum drum machine.

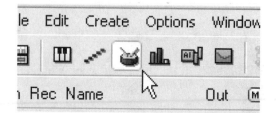

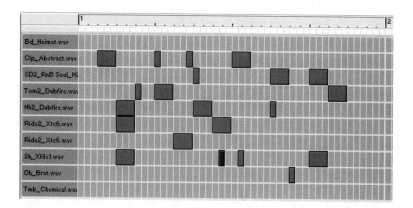

The Velocity Lane

Using a bar chart icon, the Velocity lane works with many sound modules. Depending on the device, velocity can represent different parameters. Generally speaking, velocity can be defined as the range of how soft or hard you play notes on a keyboard (or strike a part of the drum kit). In this sense, velocity will affect volume and brightness. During the course of editing our song (and depending on the sound module), it would make sense to use this lane in conjunction with the Key lane, the REX lane or the Drum lane.

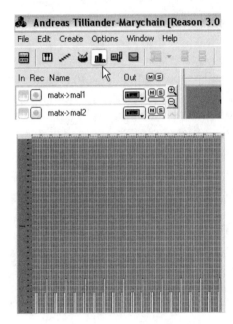

The Pattern Lane

The Pattern lane shows and allows you to edit data related to pattern-based devices such as Redrum and the Matrix.

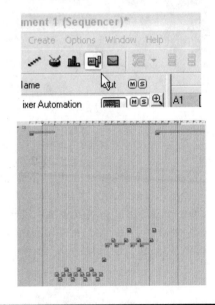

The Controller Lane

The final lane button (whose icon looks like a blue envelope) is called the Controller lane. As we compose our song, we may choose the option of automating certain parameters on different devices. Within this lane we see and can edit the data that control the device. Clicking on the Controller lane button activates three more associated buttons located to the immediate right of it.

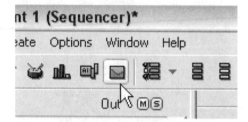

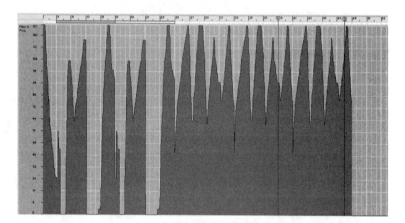

- **Controllers** – Clicking on this button will reveal a pull-down list of all possible controllers available to be used within Reason 3.0. (There are dozens.) Here you can choose to Hide or Show All Device Controllers or show just the device controllers specific to the selected track. If there is a particular controller lane being used in that track, it will be indicated by having an asterisk next to it.

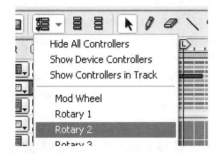

- **Show Device Controllers** – Clicking on this button will create a lane for every single controller available in Reason.

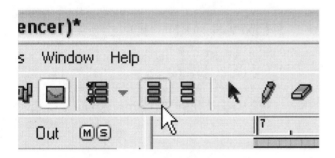

- **Show Controllers in Track** – Selecting this button will show only the controllers specifically being used by that track.

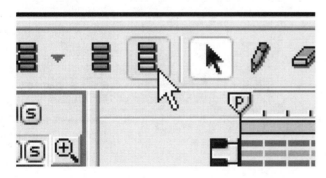

The Selection Tool

With an icon identical to the standard "pointer" cursor, the Selection tool can highlight grouped MIDI events or individual notes with ease. Selecting groups allows you to move them around and arrange them in any fashion you wish, creating the foundation for your song. Let's explore the Selection tool and other functions related to it, using our default song.

Selecting and Deselecting a Group by Clicking

1. Click on the Arrange/Edit mode button to toggle to Arrange mode.

2. Click on the Selection tool. The icon on the toolbar is depressed.

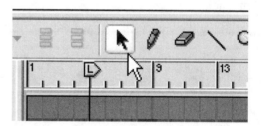

3. Find and click once on one of the groups in any track (for example, the green box in the After 6 Track). The box becomes darkened, and a small black box (called a handle) appears to the right of the group.

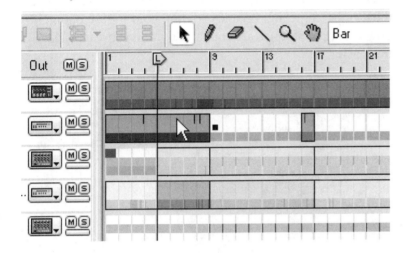

4. Click in any white area of the track. The group becomes deselected.

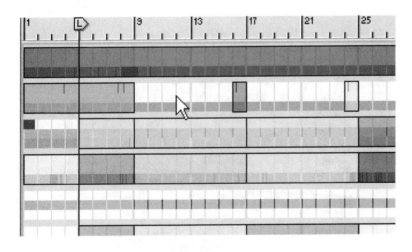

Selecting and Deselecting Using a Marquee

1. Repeat instructions 1 and 2 from the previous example.

2. On the After 6 track, click in the white area next to one of the groups (a green box) and, holding your mouse button down, drag a marquee around it. (Zoom in if it will make this easier.)

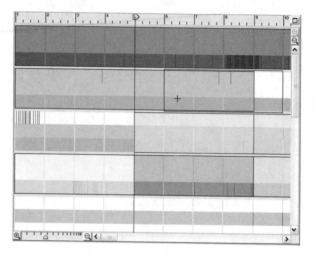

3. The box is selected and becomes darkened, and a small black box (called a handle) appears to the right of the group.

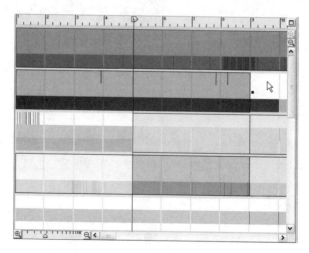

4. Click in any white area of the track. The group becomes deselected.

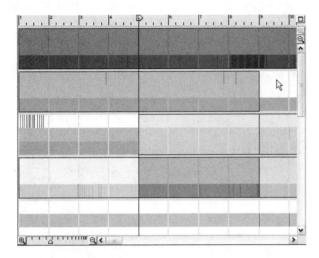

Getting a Handle on Handles

As described previously, handles are small black boxes that appear to the immediate right of a group (or a note). By grabbing the handle of a selected group and dragging left or right, you can alter the region of MIDI events that the group is governing. Try this:

1. Click on the Selection tool, then click on a group to highlight it.

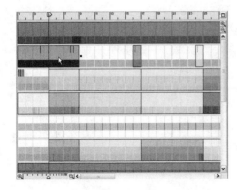

2. Click and hold your mouse button and drag the group to an area on the track not bordered by another group so there is blank (white) track on both sides. (We're just moving the group to isolate it for the sake of illustration.)

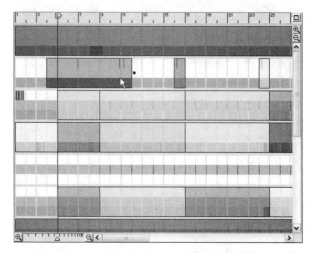

3. Click on the handle of the selected group and drag to the left. The group is now smaller, and MIDI events can be seen outside the group.

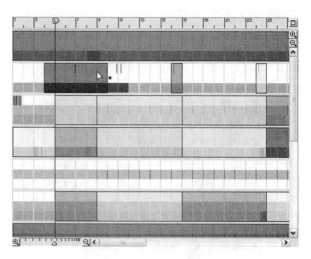

4. Click the handle and drag to the right. You now have included those MIDI events in your group and some additional space.

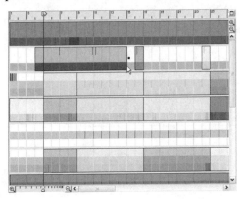

Selecting and Deselecting Multiple Groups by Clicking

1. Click on the Arrange/Edit mode button to toggle to Arrange mode.

2. Click on the Selection tool. The icon on the toolbar is depressed.

3. Holding down the Shift button, click once on a few of the of the groups (reddish-pink boxes) on the After 6 track. Each box becomes darkened, and a black handle box appears to the right of every group.

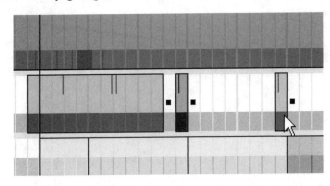

4. Click in any white area of the track. The multiple groups become deselected.

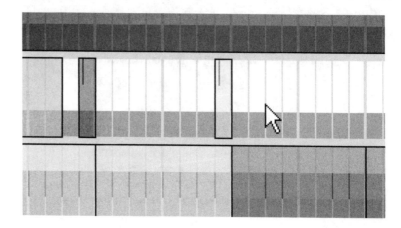

Selecting and Deselecting Multiple Groups Using a Marquee

1. Click on the Arrange/Edit mode button to toggle to Arrange mode.

2. Click on the Selection tool. The icon on the toolbar is depressed.

3. Click and hold the mouse button down in one of the white areas on the After 6 track and drag a marquee around a few of the groups (a reddish-pink boxes). Each box becomes darkened and a small black handle box appears to the right of every group.

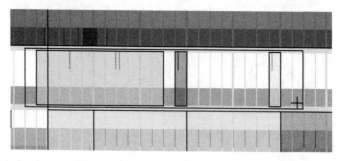

4. Click in any white area of the track. The multiple groups become deselected.

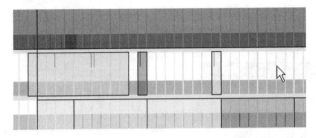

Unifying Multiple Groups into a Single Group

1. Using one of the methods outlined previously, select multiple groups.

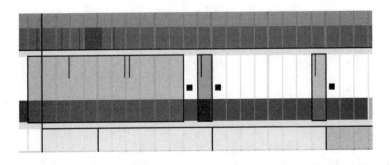

2. With your cursor over one of the selected groups, right click your mouse. A pull-down menu will appear. Choose the Group selection.

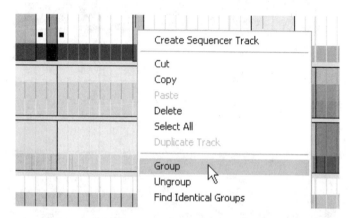

3. All of your selections will now be bounded by a single box, which represents your new single group.

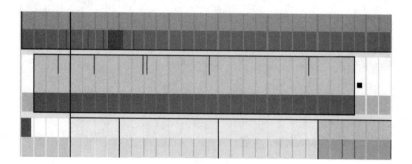

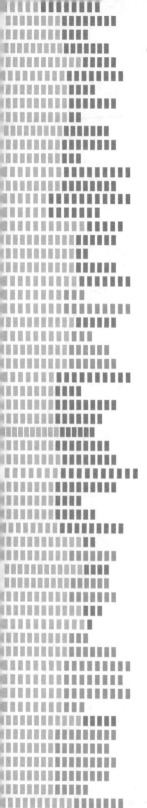

Ungrouping to Reveal MIDI Events

1. Click on a single group, then right click your mouse button. A pull-down menu will appear. Choose the Ungroup selection.

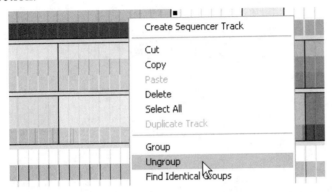

2. The color-filled box will disappear, and small, thin red vertical lines representing the MIDI events can now be seen.

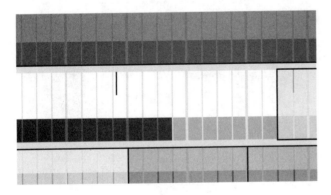

Combining MIDI Events to Create a Group

1. Use the Selection tool to drag a marquee around the MIDI events you just revealed. If you can't see them, select the Magnify tool and click on the track until they become visible.

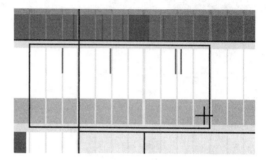

2. The selected MIDI events (vertical lines) will change to black. Position your cursor over the lines and right click to reveal the menu, then select Group.

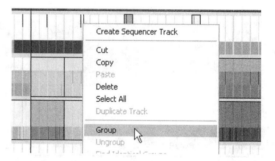

3. The MIDI events are now grouped and represented by a colored box.

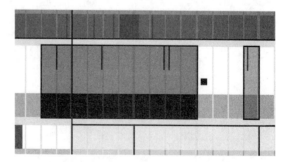

Cutting, Pasting, Copying, Moving and Deleting Groups

As you can see by our examination of the Selection tool, working with groups is child's play. The whole point of putting MIDI events together in groups is to make the work of building your song easier. Groups are designed to be dealt with as simply as text in a word processor. Groups can be cut, pasted, copied and deleted using the standard keyboard shortcuts via the Edit menu or by right clicking the selected group and choosing the option you'd like from the menu.

CUT – CTRL/COMMAND + X

PASTE – CTRL/COMMAND + V

COPY – CTRL/COMMAND + C

DELETE – Delete Key

MOVE – Grab a selected group with your mouse and drag it to the desired location. (This also works for multiply-selected groups.)

The Pencil Tool

The Pencil tool allows you to start composing within the sequencer. Using this tool, you can draw in notes and MIDI events as well as velocity and controller information. Let's trying playing around with the Pencil tool.

1. Detach the sequencer if you desire.

2. From the Track Name column in the sequencer, select the HipHop Lead track by clicking on it once. It will become highlighted.

3. Click on the Arrange/Edit mode button to toggle to Edit mode.

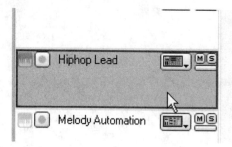

4. Activate the Key and Velocity lanes by clicking on those buttons in the toolbar.

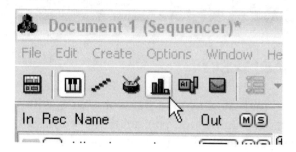

5. Click on the Pencil tool button in the toolbar.

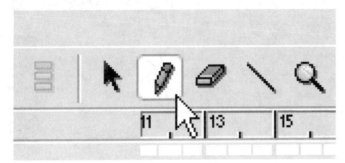

6. Click and drag your mouse around in the Key lane. You are now creating notes. Notice that when you create a note, a vertical bar also appears in the Velocity lane.

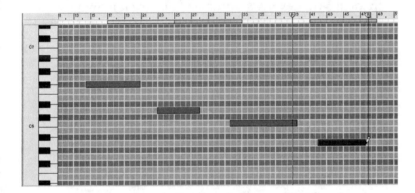

7. Click and hold your mouse button down over one of the vertical bars in the Velocity lane, then drag up or down. This is how you use the Pencil tool to affect the Velocity value.

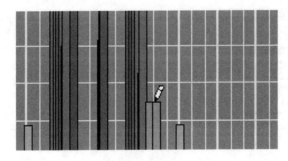

Handles

As with a group, when you select a note, a handle also appears. By clicking and holding your mouse, then dragging left or right, you can decrease or increase the duration of the note.

The Eraser Tool

Everyone makes mistakes. When you've gone a little bit haywire with the Pencil tool, you can easily correct your mistakes with the Eraser tool. This can be used to delete individual MIDI events or groups. Let's try removing some of the notes and velocity information we just created.

1. Click on the Eraser Tool button in the toolbar.

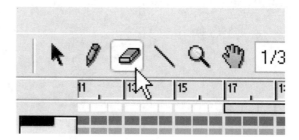

2. Find a note you created in the previous example and click on it. It is deleted.

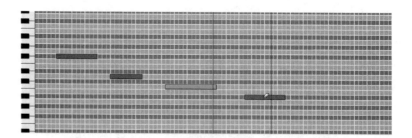

3. Now try clicking and holding the mouse button and dragging a marquee around a group of notes. When you release the mouse button, they are deleted. The same will work for the velocity information.

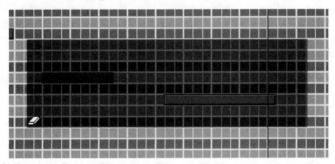

4. Click on the Arrange/Edit mode button to toggle back to Arrange mode.

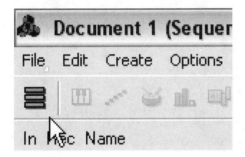

5. Click on a group in any track. That group is deleted.

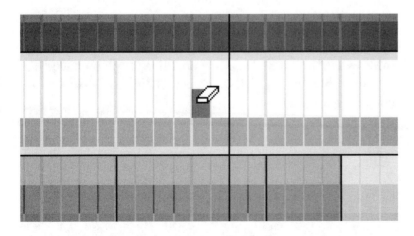

6. Click and hold your mouse button and drag a marquee around a few groups. When you release the mouse button, they are deleted.

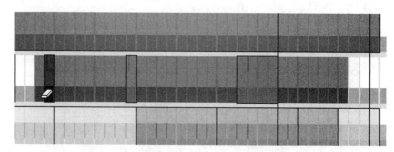

Notes

Notes can be manipulated with the Selection tool in the exact same way as groups. Once selected, notes can be moved around, cut, pasted, copied and deleted (and even grouped together) using the same methods and set of commands that work with groups.

The Line Tool

In the same way that the Pencil tool can draw individual MIDI events, the Line tool allows us to draw a series of these events in a straight or diagonal line. Typically, we will use this tool to change MIDI events relating to velocity or controller information.

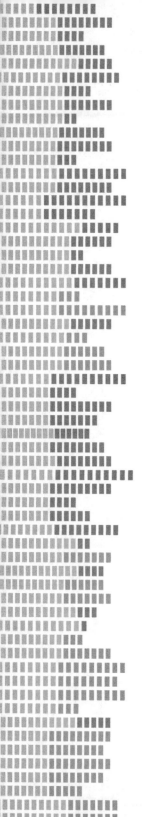

Drawing a Vertical Line to Adjust Velocity

1. Click on the Arrange/Edit mode button to toggle to Edit mode. Use the same track you had selected before, HipHop Lead.

2. Make sure that the Velocity lane is selected.

3. Click on the Line tool in the toolbar.

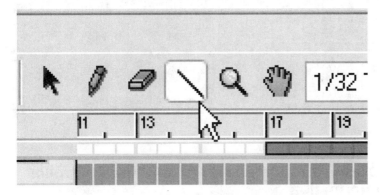

4. Position your cursor over one of the vertical bars in the Velocity lane. Click and hold your mouse button and drag downward to draw a line, then release the mouse button. The velocity of that event is decreased.

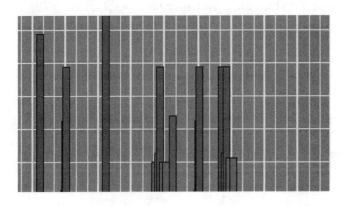

6. Click and hold your mouse button and drag upward to draw a line, then release the mouse button. The velocity is now increased for that event.

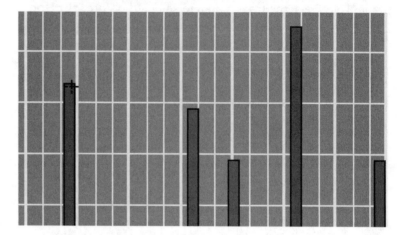

Drawing a Diagonal Line to Adjust Controller Information

1. Click on the Arrange/Edit mode button to toggle to Edit mode.

2. Make sure that the Controller lane is selected.

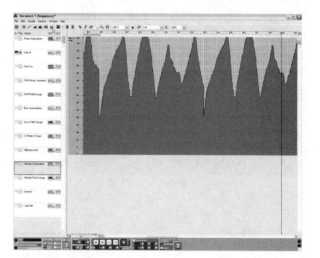

3. Select the Melody Automation track, then expand the Controller lane.

4. Click on the Line tool in the toolbar.

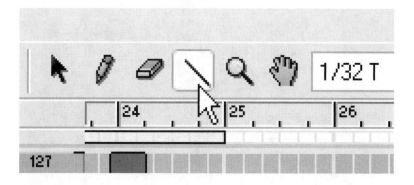

5. Position your cursor over one of the vertical bars in the Controller lane.

6. Click and hold your mouse button and drag upward and to the right to draw a diagonal line, then release the mouse button. We have adjusted the controller information over a period of time.

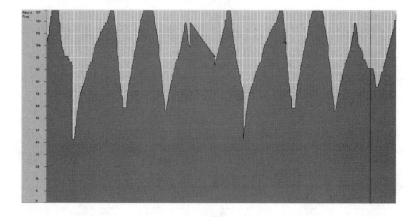

7. Click and hold your mouse button and drag downward and to the left to draw a diagonal line, then release the mouse button. We have adjusted the controller information over a period of time.

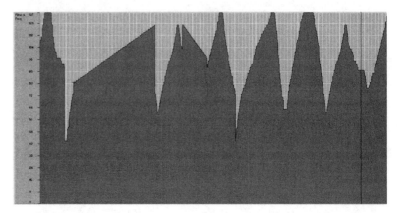

The Hand Tool

The Hand tool functions as a manual (pardon the pun) dual scroll bar. Using this tool, you can scroll both vertically across time and horizontally across the tracks – and you can do it simultaneously whether in Edit or Arrange mode.

Scrolling Horizontally Across the Timeline

1. Click on the Magnify tool and zoom in as far as you can by clicking repeatedly on a random track.

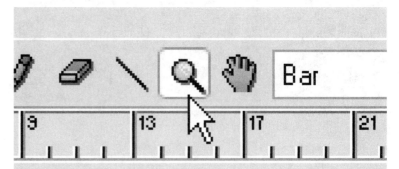

2. Click on the Hand tool to select it. Notice that in the timeline (or in the lanes) the cursor changes to a hand.

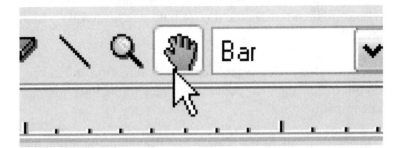

3. Click and hold the mouse button down and drag from left to right, then release the mouse button. You scroll to the left.

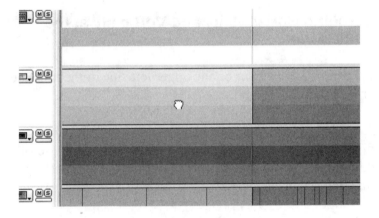

4. If you'd like to keep scrolling in this direction and have run out of space, move your cursor back to the left side and repeat instruction 4.

5. Move your cursor to the right side and use the method you just learned to scroll from right to left.

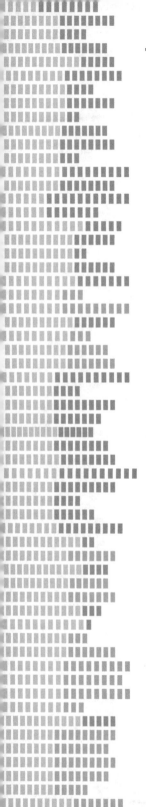

Scrolling Vertically Across the Tracks

1. Click and hold the mouse button down and drag from top to bottom, then release the mouse button. You scroll upward.

2. If you'd like to keep scrolling in this direction and have run out of space, move your cursor back to the top and repeat instruction 1.

3. Move your cursor the bottom and use the method you just learned to scroll downward.

Scrolling Horizontally and Vertically at the Same Time

1. Position your cursor on the upper left side of the timeline or lane track.

2. Click and hold the mouse button down and drag in a diagonal direction from top left to bottom right. You scroll downward through the tracks and to the right across the timeline.

3. Use this method to scroll simultaneously across both tracks and the timeline.

The Grid Size Menu

Linked to the Measure bar, this pull-down menu (to the right of the Hand tool) allows you to create a grid within the timeline. There are ten time interval increments that you can select, from as large as a bar to as small as a 1/64th note. You can set separate values for the Lane and Track views.

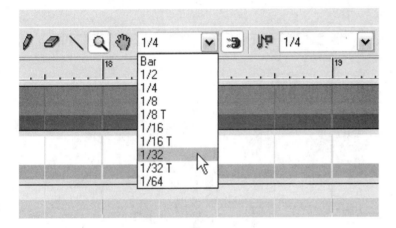

Snap to Grid Button

Just past the Grid Size menu is an icon that looks like a magnet. This is the Snap to Grid button. Based on the size of grid that you've chosen, selecting this button means that any group or event that you move will automatically align itself (snap to) the next increment. Let's see this in action.

1. Click on the Grid Size menu and select an increment of ¼ or ½ note.

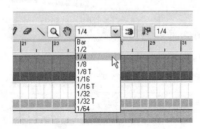

2. Click on the Snap to Grid button.

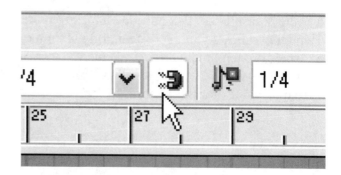

3. Click on the Selection tool.

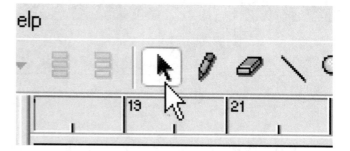

4. Click and hold the mouse button down over a group or MIDI event and slowly drag it left or right. Notice it always jumps to the next increment.

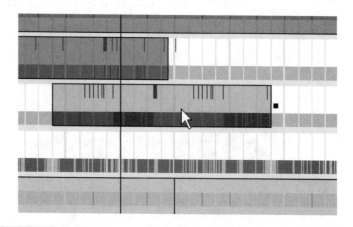

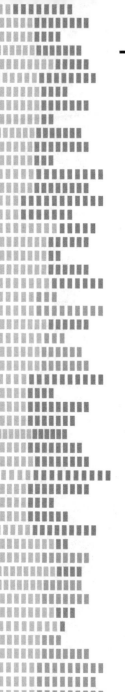

5. Click on the Snap to Grid button to deselect it.

6. Now go back to the group or MIDI event you had selected and, by clicking and holding your mouse button, try dragging it left or right. It no longer "snaps to" the next increment.

Quantize Notes During Recording

There's an old adage that says timing is everything. For most things it's true. For creating musical arrangements it's the essence of the craft. One might describe quantizing as a kind of "snap to" function. What it does is correct timing mistakes. Even experienced musicians sometimes have problems when it comes to keeping things in perfect time. When you have a MIDI device hooked up and are recording in Reason 3.0, selecting this button will ensure that any discrepancies in timing will be corrected to the nearest beat.

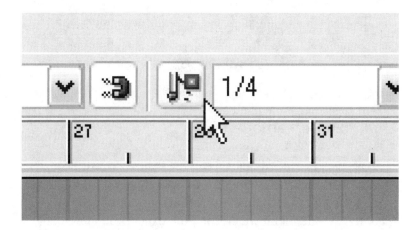

Quantize Value Menu

The value we select from this menu will determine the amount of correction for notes that are off in timing. The smaller the increment, the more "on time" the notes will be. As well as note time values we can select options for user-created quantization values (called Grooves) as well as a shuffle option that works in a way similar to the Shuffle Pattern knob on the Reason transport.

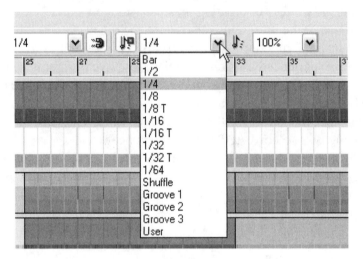

Quantize Percentage Menu

Yes, we've concluded that timing means everything. But, exactly how close in timing are we talking about? This menu gives us a way to fine tune our timing corrections. In the Quantize Value menu we defined the exact time increment we wanted the problem notes to be adjusted to. In this menu we indicate by what percentage of that increment we want the note moved. A 100% value means we want the notes moved to the closest exact quantize value. A 50% selection means we want the notes moved only half of the way to that point.

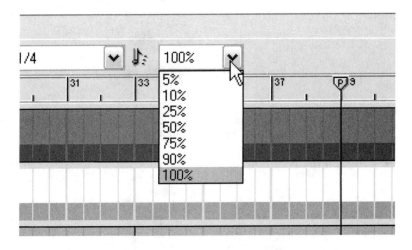

Quantize Notes

Clicking on this button will quantize or correct a series of
notes that we have selected in the sequencer.

1. Click on the Quantize Value menu and select a value, let's
say ¼ .

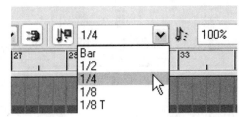

2. Click on the Quantize Percentage menu and select a value,
in this case 25%.

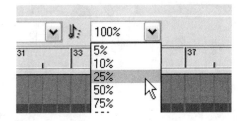

3.Click on the Arrange/Edit mode button to toggle to Edit mode.

4. Click on the Key lane button.

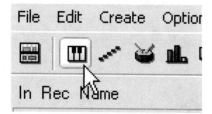

5. Select a track and expand the Key lane if necessary.

6. Make sure the Snap To button is deselected.

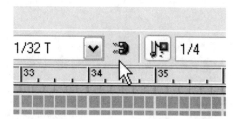

7. Click on the Selection tool.

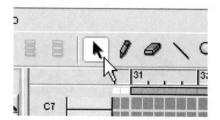

8. Using the shift click or by marquee method, select a few notes.

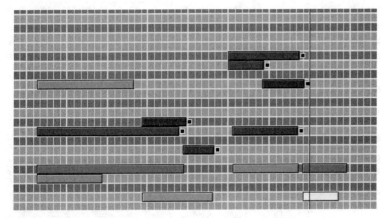

9. Clicking and holding your mouse button, move the selected notes to the left or the right by a small amount.

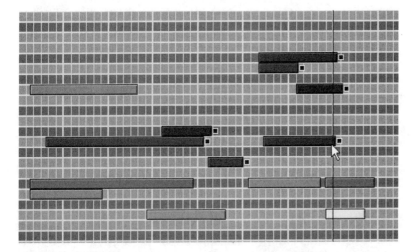

10. If you wish, repeat Steps 8 and 9 to grab and move more notes.

11. Draw a marquee around all the notes you just moved.

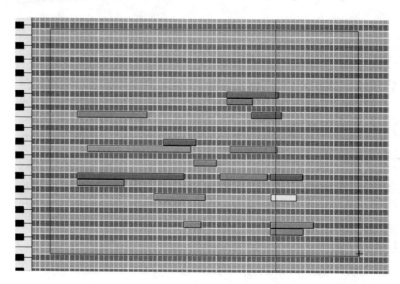

12. Click on the Quantize Notes button in the toolbar. The notes that are not in time are shifted to the closest quantizing value you selected.

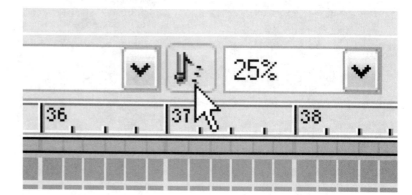

The Mixer

4

Probably one of the most recognizable pieces of audio equipment, even to those who are not professional technicians or engineers, is the mixing board. With its array of sliders, faders, knobs and small buttons, it can appear to be very intimidating, but it isn't as complicated as it appears. The focus of this chapter is the Reason 3.0 Mixer, and we will cover every part of it, on *both* sides, front and back! Once we learn the basics of the mixer, we'll spin off into learning how effects relate to the tracks, as well as the two methods for adding effects. We'll also discuss how devices are incorporated into the board and learn something about audio routing. In this chapter we'll cover:

- **The Channel Strip Controls**

- **Send and Insert Methods of Adding Effects**

- **Signal Flow**

- **Working with Modules & Devices**

- **Creating an Insert Effect**

Introduction to the Reason 3.0 Mixer (a.k.a. Mixer 14:2)

Let's start off with a basic question... what exactly is a mixer? On its simplest level, a mixer is a device that takes multiple audio signal inputs and then routes them, changes their levels, dynamics and tones, and finally (but most importantly) combines (or sums) them into a unified output. Makes sense, doesn't it? Specifically, Reason 3.0's mixer allows you to control:

- The Audio Level (volume)

- The Stereo Placement (pan direction)

- The Tone (equalization)

- The Effect Mix (auxiliary sends)

The Reason 3.0 mixer has another name. It's also called Mixer 14:2. Why 14:2? Because it has 14 stereo input channels that are combined to output through two master channels (left and right).

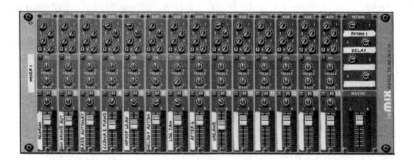

The Channel Strips

Part of what seems to make the mixer so intimidating is the multitude of knobs, buttons, sliders and meters all over the place. Things will seem much more basic when we break the mixer down into its essential parts. Find the mixer on the Reason 3.0 interface and look at the top left side of it. You'll see two virtual screws with the letters AUX between them. Looking down, you'll see four red knobs. Then you'll see below that two blue knobs, one grey knob and finally at the very bottom a slider (called a fader). What you've just passed your eyes over is called a "channel strip." And if you examine the mixer, what you'll find is that it's really 14 channel strips. When you look at it that way, it doesn't seem so complicated at all.

The Channel Strip Controls

Just a short time ago we covered the general functions that the mixer is capable of performing (volume, pan, EQ and auxiliary sends). We can access all of these via the channel strip controls. Let's work our way from bottom to top.

Channel Fader

The "channel fader" is a slider at the very bottom of the control strip. It controls the output volume (also called "level") of the device or sound module you have connected to that channel. Adjusting the level is the essence of sound mixing. By balancing the levels of the different channels, you create the mix for your song. Adjusting the faders is very basic.

1. Position your mouse pointer over the fader.

2. Click and hold down the mouse button and slide the pointer up and down. The fader moves in the direction you select, up for increasing the level and down for decreasing it. Also, a red box will appear indicating the channel number

and a numeric value (from zero to 127) representing the volume.

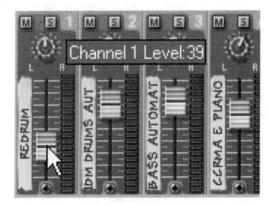

Channel Meter

To the right of the fader is the "channel meter." Everyone will be familiar with this, as almost every audio component from consumer to professional these days has some sort of visual representation of output level. The way it works is very simple: the more lights visible, the louder your output level is.

Getting Out of the Red

It's a good idea to stay out of the red in your channel meter. Seeing red means that you've set the level too high, and this may result in clipping. Pull your fader down to correct this.

Channel Label

To the left of the fader is the "channel label," indicating the
name of the device that is connected to the channel strip. The
name shown on the label is read only and cannot be altered
in the mixer.

Pan Knob

The first knob we see above the fader is the Pan knob. Pan is
used to control the position of a single sound channel
between left and right stereo outputs. When pan is in the
neutral or center position, we hear sound from both left and
right sources equally. By adjusting the pan we can "move"
the sound anywhere in the range from all the way to the left
to all the way to the right.

1. Position your mouse pointer over the Pan knob.

2. Click and hold down the mouse button and slide the pointer down. This will turn the knob to the left. A red box will appear indicating the channel number and a pan value (from -1 to -64). This represents the degree to which you have moved the sound to the left.

3. Click and hold down the mouse button and slide the pointer up. This will turn the knob to the right. A red box will appear. This indicates the channel number and a pan value (from +1 to +64) representing the degree to which you have moved the sound to the right.

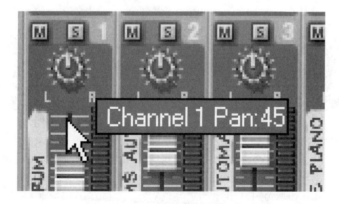

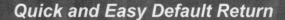

Quick and Easy Default Return

If you've made adjustments to a few knobs and would like to reset them to the neutral position, it's very easy. Holding down the CTRL (Mac-COMMAND) button, click once on the knob, and it will return to zero position.

Mute and Solo Buttons

While it's great to hear the built-in demo song that Reason 3.0 has provided in its entirety, we can't learn much about how the song was built without being able to isolate its different tracks and listen to them. The two buttons that allow us to accomplish this are the Mute and Solo buttons found just above the Pan knob.

1. Position your mouse pointer over the Solo button and click once. It becomes highlighted in green. Notice that the Mute button on every other track is highlighted in red.

2. Press the space bar or the Play button in the transport. You now hear only that track being played. Notice also that only the channel meter for the track you have soloed is showing output levels.

3. Try turning on the Solo button for a few more tracks and listen to get a feel of how each track interacts with the other.

Some Mute and Solo Facts and Tips

When you turn on solo for a channel, all other channels are automatically muted. You can't mute a soloed channel. Click on the Solo button to turn it off. Then you can mute it. When no channels are soloed, all are enabled.

EQ Buttons

The first set of filters we can apply to our audio signal uses a pair of EQ knobs. You activate these controls by clicking on the EQ button, which will highlight red when selected. The Treble knob allows us either to cut or boost the higher frequencies of the audio on our channel while the Bass knob can be used to adjust the lower frequencies.

1. Click on the EQ button to activate the two knobs.

2. Solo your track and press space bar to play.

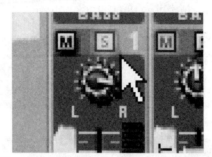

3. Position your mouse pointer over the Treble knob and then click and hold your mouse button down.

4. Pull your mouse down to turn the knob to the left. A red box appears and tells us the amount (as a negative value) by which we are cutting the higher frequencies of this channel. Note the sound of the effect the more you cut the EQ.

5. Slide the pointer upward to turn the knob to the right. A red box appears and tells us the amount (as a positive value) by which we are boosting the higher frequencies of this channel. Again, note the sound of the effect as you increasingly raise the EQ.

6. Repeat instructions 3 to 5 using the Bass knob.

7. Toggle the EQ button on and off to listen to the difference between your EQ filtered sound and the original sound of the track. (By the way, the term for this - when we choose to ignore the parameters we have set and listen to the raw (or dry) signal – is called "bypassing.")

What Exactly Is EQ?

EQ is a shortened version of the word Equalization. We "do" equalization on a device called an equalizer. Basically, what an equalizer does is raise or lower (a.k.a. boost or cut) a specific frequency or range of frequencies. There are many different kinds of equalizers out there, and Reason 3.0 has a sound module called the PEQ-2 Two Band Parametric Equalizer for additional EQ abilities outside of the mixer.

Old and New EQ

If you wish to play back a song that was created on an earlier version of Reason, the EQ mode may not be compatible, and the song won't sound exactly the same. To correct this, Reason 3.0 allows you to switch to a mode that will make the old song's EQ mode compatible.

1. Press the Tab key or go to the Options menu and select Toggle Rack Front/Rear. You will now see the cabling at the back of the mixer.

2. At the bottom left (just above the reMIX label) is a switch that has two settings: Compatible EQ and Improved EQ. Move your pointer over the button and click to toggle it to the Compatible EQ setting to ensure that older songs can play on Reason 3.0 without altered EQ. Press Tab to flip the rack back around.

AUX Send

At the very top of the channel strip are four red knobs and a small button with a letter "P" on it. These are the Auxiliary Send knobs and the Pre-Fader button. The Send knobs allow you to "send" part of the signal routed through your channel strip out to up to four auxiliary devices. Why would we want to do this? Mostly to use effects. By sending our signal out of the mixer we can take advantage of all the features available in the many high end effects processors offered in Reason 3.0. By turning up any of the AUX Send knobs you are indicating how large a portion of the signal you wish to send out.

Return (AUX Return)

A moment ago we talked about the knobs at the top of our channel strip. These AUX Sends are technically outputs, as they "send" the signal out of the mixer to an auxiliary device. What happens to the audio signal once it's been modified by the effects device? Well, it needs to "return" (be input) back to re:MIX so we can incorporate it into our mix. So the returns can be seen as inputs. The function of each Return knob (and we can return from up to four devices we "send" to) is to determine how much we will blend the level of our returned (effected) signal with the original signal. Notice on the mixer that each return has a read-only label that tells you the name of the specific effects device the signal is returning from, as well as a knob to adjust the blend level. Let's examine how this works by isolating one track in our built-in song and sending its signal out to be effected, then return it to the mixer.

1. Position your mouse pointer over the Solo button of Track 1 (called Redrum) and click once. It becomes highlighted in green. We are now soloing the drum track.

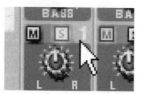

2. In the sequencer, press the play button or hit the space bar. You should now hear your drum track only playing.

3. Adjust the Reason interface to reveal the device immediately below the mixer, called the RV-7000 Advanced Reverb device. Notice that this device is shown on the label for the first return channel.

4. Position your mouse pointer over the top (first) knob in the AUX portion of the channel strip. Click and hold this button down and push your pointer up (turning the knob to the right) until you start to hear the drum track with reverb effect applied.

5. Position your mouse pointer over the top (first) knob in the return portion of the Mixer. Click and hold the mouse button down and push your pointer up (turning the knob to the right). Notice that if you turn the knob all the way to the right, you hear a strongly effected version of the signal, while if you turn the knob all the way to the left, it is unaffected. Adjust the knob to find the best blend.

6. For curiosity's sake, try experimenting by adjusting a few of the knobs on the RV-7000. You will hear the reverb of your signal change in real time as you turn the knobs.

7. If your audio starts clipping, click and hold the fader on channel strip one and slide your mouse button down to lower the level. This is an example of how you'd use the Aux Send and Return to incorporate effects into your mix.

A Note on Sending and Returning

Something that may seem obvious but is at times overlooked is that no matter how high you decide to set your AUX Return, you will not hear any effected signal unless you send out (turn up) your AUX Send. Also, if you have your Send turned full to the right but the corresponding Return turned all the way to the left, you will only hear only the original signal with no effects on it.

Signal Flow

As we are beginning to study how auxiliary sends and returns work, it's a good time to introduce signal flow. What is signal flow? It's the pathway navigated by the audio signal as it travels through the channel strip and mixer and various audio components. Since we've learned the functions of the channel strip, let's see how the audio signal travels through it.

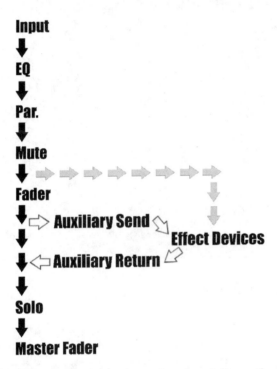

The black arrow path shows how the signal flows through the channel strip if you are choosing not to use the auxiliary sends. Notice that the routing of the signal is not identical to the actual layout of the channel strip. The white arrow path shows us how the signal flows when utilizing the auxiliary sends and returns to add effects. The signal is returned to the hierarchy before the Solo button. That means you adjust the final level of the effected audio with the fader for that channel.

What's This Method Called?

What we've learned so far regarding using the AUX Sends and Returns is only one way to incorporate effects. Logically, this is called the send method. We use this method when we want a portion of the audio signal to be effected. The benefit is that we can apply up to four different effect processors to one channel. In addition, other channels on the mixer can also utilize these effects.

Not all effects are best utilized via the send method. The PEQ2 Parametric Equalizer and the Comp-01 Compressor were designed to be used to insert effects. When you insert effects, you allow the whole signal to be passed through the effect (as opposed to sending only part of it, as takes place in the send method.) We will explain the insert effects option in more detail shortly.

Pre-Fader Button

The gray arrow path on the signal path diagram shows us how we can use the Pre-Fader button to create an insert effect. The Pre-Fader button is located below and to the right of the AUX Send knobs. Depressing this button allows us to use the fourth Send button as an effect fader. As with an insert effect, we can hear what the whole signal sounds like when it is passed through the effect. Let's examine this using our built-in song.

1. Right click in the empty area of the rack next to the DDL-1 component to bring up a pull-down menu. Select RV7000 Advanced Reverb.

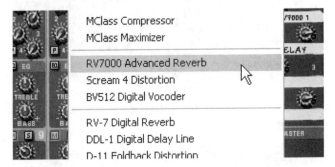

2. Repeat Instruction 1. Notice in the return portion of the mixer that Returns 3 and 4 now have labels showing the RV-7000.

3. Position your mouse pointer over the Solo button of Track 1 (called Drums) and click once. It turns green. We are now soloing the drum track.

4. In the sequencer click Play or press the space bar.

5. Position your mouse over the "P" Pre-Fader button and press once to activate it. It will turn red.

6. Turn the Aux Send 4 button to the right so it is at the 3 o'clock position.

7. Turn the Aux Return 4 button to the right so it is at 3 o'clock.

8. Position your pointer over the channel one fader and hold the mouse button down. Drag downward until the fader is at the very bottom.

When the fader was up, you still heard the original track blended with the effect track, but now you are hearing the entire signal effected by the RV-7000 Advance Reverb effect processor.

Master Fader

The last item on the mixer to examine is the "master fader." This is the final output that controls the overall left and right levels of your mix before the signal is sent to your audio hardware.

The Line Mixer 6:2 (a.k.a. microMIX)

New to Reason 3.0 is the "mini-me" version of the reMIX, which is called the Line Mixer 6:2. It is essentially a very scaled down version of its bigger sibling. The features of the microMIX include:

- Six stereo mixing channels
- Knobs instead of faders for controlling volume level
- Standard Solo and Mute buttons
- Standard Pan knob

134

Starting Something from Nothing

Let's try beginning from a completely clean slate to set up the building blocks for creating a song.

1. Go to the File menu and select New or press CTRL (Command key on a Mac) + N. A new interface appears.

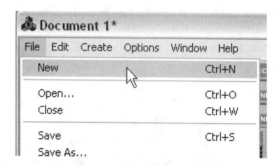

Adding the Mixer (or any device) to the Rack

There are two ways to add a device to the rack and they are quite easy. Let's add our main mixer.

1. Click the Create menu and select SubTractor Analog Synthesizer. The synth appears in the rack. Alternatively, you can position your pointer in an empty area of the rack, and click and hold your right mouse button. A pull-down menu appears. Select Mixer 14:2. You now have two mixers on your rack!

Removing a Device from the Rack

Let's get rid of one of our mixers using one of three methods.

1. Click at the far left of the SubTractor, anywhere between the two virtual screws. The mixer is highlighted by a grey box that bounds it.

2. Go to the Edit pull-down menu and select Delete Device.

OR

3. Click at the far left of the mixer, anywhere between the two virtual screws. The mixer is highlighted by a grey box that bounds it.

4. Click on your mouse's right button and from the pull-down menu that appears select delete device.

OR

3. Click at the far left of the mixer, anywhere between the two virtual screws. The mixer is highlighted by a grey box that bounds it.

4. Hold down the CTRL (Mac: Command) button, then press the Delete button. The mixer is deleted.

More Device Moving Options

Just like text in a word processor, devices in Reason can be cut, copied and pasted.

Moving a Device in the Rack

Let's add a few more devices to illustrate how to do this.

1. Using one of the methods you learned earlier, add two devices to rack: the Dr:Rex loop player and the PH-90 Phaser.

2. Move your pointer to the far left of the PH-90 Phaser between the screws. Click and hold the mouse button down. The device is bordered by a red box.

3. Drag upwards to between the Dr:Rex and the Mixer. As you drag, a red box will appear. When you reach that point, a thick red line will appear between the two devices.

4. Release the mouse button. The PH-90 unit has now been moved between the Mixer and the Dr:Rex. As an exercise, use this method to return the Dr.Rex loop player to its original position.

Hiding a Device in the Rack

As you develop your song, you will involve more and more devices. There is an easy method to hide devices you're not currently using.

1. Move your pointer to the far left of the PH-90 between the screws. Click once on the arrow icon. The device is now "minimized" or hidden on the rack.

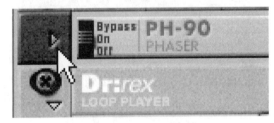

2. Try the same with the Dr:Rex loop player.

3. Click once on the arrow icon for both devices. They are now fully visible in the rack.

Naming a Device in the Rack

What's in a name? Well, pretty much everything! Part of being well organized within Reason 3.0 is labeling devices. This will come in very handy when you have multiples of the same device. Labeling is simple!

1. Click once on the name tag of the PH-90 where it says PHASER 1.

2, Type in the text "Super Phaser" and press Enter. The tag now has a new name! Notice too that in the mixer the track is named after the device.

Creating an Insert Effect

We've got the mixer, the Dr:Rex loop player and the PH-90 Phaser effect now in the rack. Let's see how these have automatically been set up and routed to create an insert effect.

1. Move your pointer to the upper left of the Dr:Rex loop player and find the Browse Loop button. (It looks like a small icon of a folder.) Click on it once.

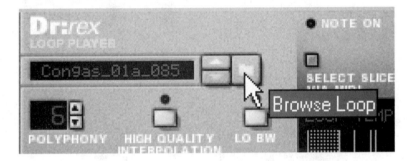

2. Under Locations, click on the Reason Factory Sound Bank. This will reveal a number of folders. Three of these – Dr:Rex Drum, Instrument or Percussion Loops – can apply to us. Feel free to browse through these folders and take advantage of the Audition function to hear what these loops sound like. For the sake of our example, I have browsed to Dr Rex Percussion Loops > Congas 085bpm > Congas_01a_85.

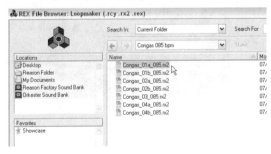

3. Click on the file, then click OK.

4. On the Dr:Rex loop player you will now see that Congas is loaded in the small window.

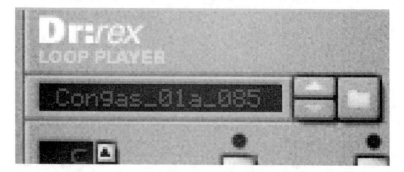

5. Go to the PH-90 Phaser unit and click and drag the button on the far left upward so it is set to Bypass.

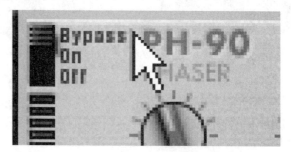

6. Return to the Dr:Rex loop player and press once on the Preview button. It plays a loop of the Congas.

7. Return to the PH-90 and move the button you just switched in instruction 5 so that it is now set to on.

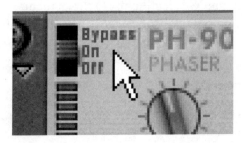

8. Manipulate a few of the dials on PH-90 and listen to the how Congas loop sounds with the phase effect applied.

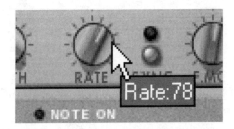

Ok, so we've applied it. But how exactly is this an insert effect? Well, for one, the way we have set this effect up to work is quite different from the way we set things up with our auxiliary sends and returns. The best way to see this, though, is to do a little looking "behind" the scenes...

Basic Routing I - Insert Effect

Routing is all about how things are wired or connected together. For those of you who have trembled at the thought of having to hook up your VCR, I'm sure your natural reaction now is to run and hide. Please don't! Routing is very straightforward with Reason 3.0, and the best part is there is no dealing with dust bunnies!

Viewing the Back of the Rack

1. So let's begin by selecting the Options menu and choosing Toggle Rack Front/Rear (or use the keyboard shortcut, which is the Tab key.)

2. We've now flipped the rack to look at the back. To see the whole interface, you may wish to completely minimize the sequencer by clicking the top of it and dragging it all the way down till all that can be seen is the Reason transport.

The Signal Path and How It's Routed

Routing is all about flow – where we choose to direct the flow of the audio signal from one point to another. It will usually originate with a device and then travel through the various sound modules in the rack until it comes out through the audio hardware. In plainest terms, it's from output to input to output and so on. Our audio signal begins with the Dr:Rex loop player. At the far right of the backside of the player are the left and right Audio Outputs. Follow the path (route) of the green cables to see where they will deliver the audio signal to next. They enter the left and right inputs of the PH-90 Phaser. Next to these are the left and right outputs. If we follow these green cables and the signal path, we'll see that they arrive at the inputs for the first channel strip on the reMIX mixer. If we look to the far right side of the mixer, we'll see two red cables that are connected to the Master Out ports of the mixer. They lead us to our final destination in Reason, which is the hardware interface. It's from here the audio signal will exit Reason to the audio card and finally out the speakers.

Another Look at the Front of the Rack

Return your view to the front of the rack. You do this by selecting the Options menu and choosing Toggle Rack Front/Rear (or use the keyboard shortcut, which is the Tab key.) Starting with the mixer, take a look at the label for channel strip 1. It's called Super Phaser, the same as the label we re-typed on the PH-90. Why? Because the phaser is the device that is connected directly to it. So even though our audio signal is being created by Dr:Rex loop player, the phaser is named on the channel strip. Look down to the sequencer. Notice that in the sequencer, the track name is called Dr:Rex1, not the Phaser. In the sequencer we are seeing the device that is "originating" the audio signal. Noting the discrepancy in names between the mixer and the sequencer we should be reminded of the importance of labeling things properly!

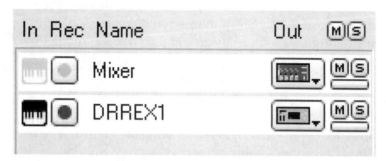

Basic Routing II - Send Effect

After that explanation of routing, hopefully your confidence has been boosted – because we're about to get our virtual hands dirty! You've noticed that devices generated in the rack can be automatically routed and patched together. This is what happened when we added the mixer, Dr:Rex loop player and PH-90 Phaser to the rack. As we saw when we flipped the rack, they were perfectly patched together for an insert effect. Now we are going to repatch them manually so that they are set up to create a send effect.

1. Start by flipping the rack. Choose the Options menu and click Toggle Rack Front/Rear or press the Tab key.

2. Let's re-route the signal path so it is coming directly from the Dr:Rex loop player to Channel 1 on the mixer. Follow the green cable that leaves the audio output L channel to where it enters the phaser (L-in). Position your pointer over the plug and click and hold your mouse button down. Drag this plug to the top most port, on Channel 1 on the mixer then release the mouse button. The cable will change in color to red.

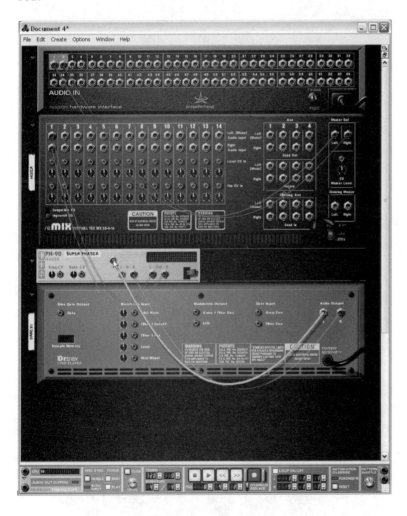

Disappearing Cables

When you select a cable in Reason 3.0 and move it, it becomes highlighted in silver, and all of the other cables become transparent. This makes it much easier to see what you are doing!

3. The original cable that was plugged into channel 1 has disappeared. Don't be concerned with this, as Reason removes what we do not need. Using the same method from instruction 2, take the cable end from the right input of the PH-90 and "plug it into" the second port, on the mixer's channel 1. We now have a direct connection from the loop player to the mixer.

4. Position your pointer over the Number 1 left Aux Send
Out port on the mixer. Click and hold the mouse button down
and drag down to the PH-90 Phaser's left In port, then release
the mouse button. Not only will Reason auto-generate a
cable, when you have placed it in the correct port it will also
create a cable and a connection from the right Aux Send
output to the right phaser input automatically!

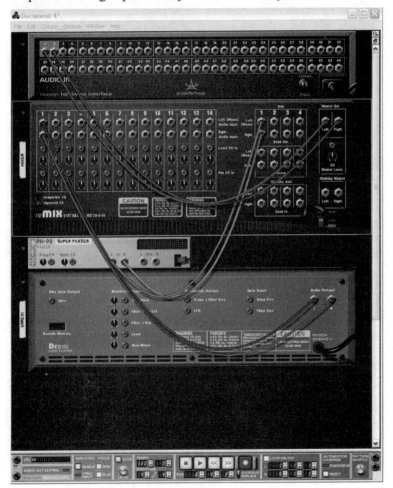

5. Go to the PH-90 Phaser unit and position your pointer over the left Out. Click and hold your mouse button down and drag up to the port for left Return. When you release the mouse button, it will automatically create a cable connection for both right and left channels from the phaser to the Aux Return.

6. Press the Tab key to flip the rack.

The Front of the Rack with a Send Effect Routing Setup

Taking a comparative glance (versus our routing setup for an insert effect), the first thing we'll notice is that the label on channel strip 1 of the mixer is now labeled as DRREX1. This of course is because the Dr:Rex loop player is now routed directly to the mixer. Notice now that in the Return portion of the mixer the first return is labeled Super Phaser. This, of course, is because of the way we routed the phaser into the auxiliary sends and returns. Finally, in the sequencer, we can see that the device listed is still DRREX1.

Reason Synthesizers 5

Congratulations on diving in and exploring some of the introductory aspects of Reason 3.0! With these basics under our belts, we can start to delve into the "meat" of the software, the sound modules. As you'll recall from our previous chapters, musical notes or MIDI events can be created right in the sequencer. While this is one way of composing your song, it is not the most typical – or natural, for that matter. If we're going to compose, the most intuitive method is to use a keyboard. In this chapter we'll cover how to integrate your keyboard into Reason 3.0 and see how it works with some sound modules.

- **Configuring Reason for MIDI Input**

- **The SubTractor Polyphonic Synthesizer in Depth**

- **Initializing a Device**

- **Saving a Patch**

- **The Malström Graintable Synthesizer in Depth**

Connecting Your Keyboard to Reason

Unlike the clean and easy way that we deal with the virtual cables at the back of the rack, connecting a keyboard to your computer means handling the real thing. Luckily, we will be handling far fewer cables than we deal with on the rack! Here's what you'll need:

- A MIDI compatible keyboard (with a MIDI OUT port)

- A MIDI cable

- A MIDI IN on your computer's audio card

- A MIDI/USB interface in case you don't have a MIDI IN on your computer

The typical audio card found in your computer will not likely have a MIDI input. In the event you don't have this connector, you can purchase a MIDI to USB interface. Essentially what this device does is allow you to plug the MIDI cable that goes out of your keyboard into the computer via a USB port.

Configuring Reason for MIDI Input - Part I

Once you have connected the keyboard to your computer, you can configure Reason to recognize it. The first thing you need to do is let Reason know what device is connected as a MIDI IN. We can define this in the Advanced MIDI settings.

1. From the Edit menu select Preferences. This opens the Preferences window.

2. From the Page menu in the Preferences window select Advanced MIDI.

3. In the Bus A: selection click on the down arrow and select the device/port that is bringing in your MIDI information.

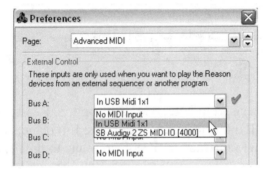

4. Close the Preferences window. Look to the top of the rack at MIDI IN Device. If it's not already selected, click on the A next to Bus Select. In the green window to the right you'll notice the name of the device that is bringing in your MIDI signal. Reason 3.0 is now configured to bring in MIDI information from your keyboard.

Configuring Reason for MIDI Input - Part II

Now that we have configured the MIDI input and bus information, we can define the keyboard that we're going to choose. We make this selection in the Control Surfaces and Keyboard settings.

1. From the Edit menu select Preferences. This opens the Preferences window.

2. From the Page menu in the Preferences window select Control Surfaces and Keyboards.

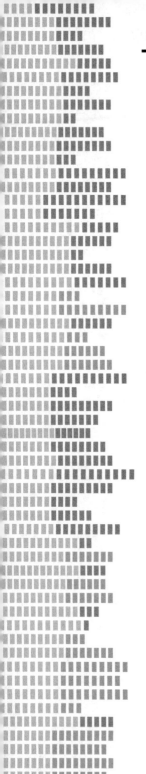

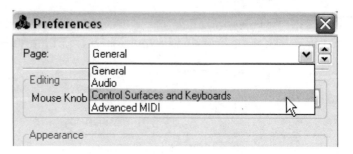

3. Click on the Auto-detect Surfaces button. Reason will scan the MIDI bus looking for devices. If it detects one, continue on to instruction. If not, continue to the next instruction.

4. Click on the Add button at the bottom of the window. This will open the Control Surfaces window.

5. Use the Manufacturer and Model pull-down menus to select your keyboard. The name will appear at the bottom of the window. If your manufacturer/model is not listed, choose Other from the Manufacturer menu and Basic MIDI Keyboard from the Model menu. The name information will now be displayed at the bottom of the window.

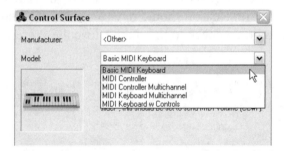

6. From the MIDI Input menu select the input to which your keyboard is connected. You may also choose to click on the Find button. If you do, this will open the Find MIDI Input window. It will ask you to press a key on your keyboard, which will determine which input is being used. Click Choose to select it. If it didn't detect, try pressing the Try Again button. Double check your connections if your input is not being detected.

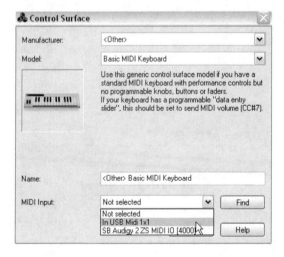

7. Once you've selected Choose, you'll be returned to the Control Surfaces window. Click OK.

8. You're now back at the Preferences window. Notice that in the Attached Surfaces part of the window there is an image of a keyboard with your manufacturer/model name as well as the words "This is the master keyboard." The box next to Use with Reason should have a check in it, and there should be a green check to the right. Close the Preferences window.

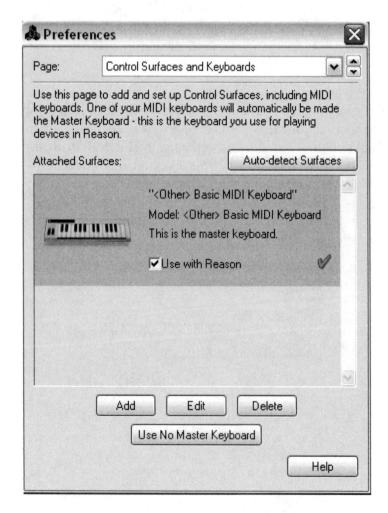

Using the Keyboard With a Sound Module

In the world of Reason 3.0, the keyboard, in and of itself, is really just an input device. To be of value, it needs to work with one of our sound modules. There are six devices with which we can use our keyboard.

- SubTractor Analog Synthesizer

- Malström Graintable Synthesizer

- NN19 Digital Sampler

- NN-XT Advanced Sampler

- Dr:Rex Loop Player

- Redrum Drum Computer

1. Start with a clean slate. Go to the File menu > New (or use the keyboard shortcut: CTRL/Command + N). We want an empty rack.

2. Click on the Combinator to select it and then press the Delete key. A dialog will prompt you, asking if you really wish to delete it. Accept the delete.

3. Right click in the empty rack area and create a 14:2 mixer if there is not already one there.

4. Right click in the empty rack area and create a SubTractor Polyphonic Synthesizer.

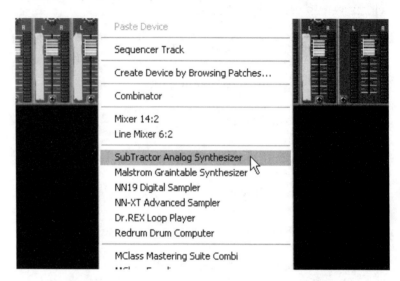

5. Start hitting a few keys on your keyboard. You're making music!!!!

Recording Music from Keyboard Input

No doubt this is the moment you've been waiting for! You've got that song in your head, and you just can't wait to get it out. The urge to compose has your fingers twitching! In a short time we'll talk about how to adjust the different devices to change the sounds you get out of your synthesizers. But for now, using the setup from our previous instructions, let's learn how to record the music we create with our keyboard. Start by looking in the Name track of the Sequencer window. Ensure that you can see the In column showing a keyboard icon and that the Record column shows a red circle. This means you are ready to record.

1. In the sequencer click on the Arrange/Edit Mode button to toggle to Edit mode.

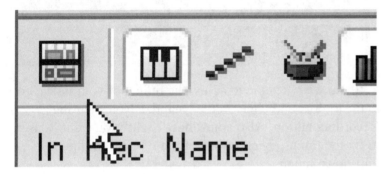

2. Detach or enlarge the sequencer timeline using one of the methods you learned earlier.

3. Click on the Show Key Lane and Show Velocity Lane buttons to activate them.

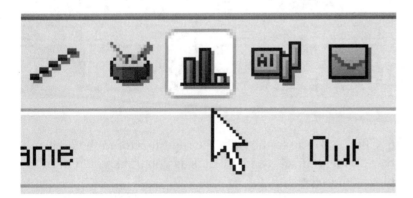

4. Placing your pointer between the two lanes in the timeline, click and hold down the mouse button and drag down to reveal most of the Key lane.

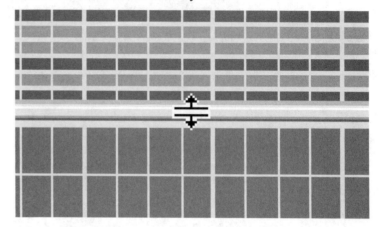

5. If you wish Reason to adjust the timing of your notes, go to the toolbar and click on the Quantize Notes During Recording button. Also adjust how "tight" you want Reason to fix the timing by choosing a time frame from the pull-down menu.

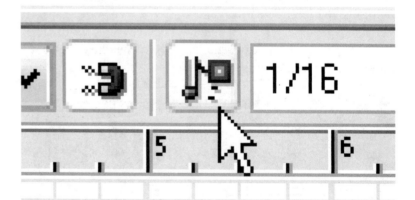

6. Click and drag to the right the right locator in the Measure bar, giving yourself as many bars as you think you'll need to play your piece.

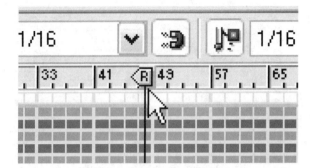

7. Underneath the Record button in the Transport bar, select the type of recording you wish to do, overdub or replace.

8. Press the Record button, then the Play button and start playing your song on your keyboard!

Congratulations! You've just recorded your first song. Let's take a look and see what you've accomplished.

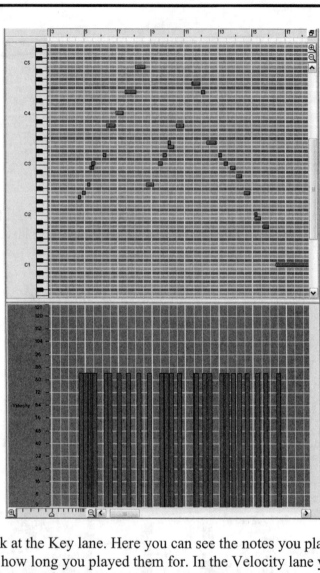

Look at the Key lane. Here you can see the notes you played and how long you played them for. In the Velocity lane you can see the speed with which you hit the keys. If you wished, you could use the tools you learned about from the toolbar to lengthen or shorten, move, delete and or even add more notes! If you toggle back to the Arrange mode (by clicking once on the Arrange/Edit Mode button), you can also see individual MIDI events that you could group together and manipulate. Now that you've learned how to use the keyboard and record, let's turn to the actual synthesizer to learn how to change the nature of your sound.

What Is a Synthesizer?

It is an electronic instrument that creates its sounds by taking an analog signal (an electrical current) and manipulating the wave-form using various techniques.

SubTractor Polyphonic Synthesizer

Welcome to the world of waves. Sound waves, that is. When we work with synthesizers, we are essentially tweaking almost every aspect of a wave-form to create unique sounds. Explaining how wave-forms can be generated, modified, warped, amplified, filtered, twisted -- and the multitude of other things that can be done to them -- can be extremely complicated. The purpose of this book is not to cover wave dynamics, although we will need to understand some aspects of what affects a wave-form in order to understand the capabilities of our synthesizer. In an attempt to keep things straightforward, let's break down the name of this particular synthesizer to understand what exactly it does. The name SubTractor indicates the type of synthesis that is being performed on the wave-form. Subtractive synthesis is a technique that creates sounds by filtering simple wave-forms, which are generated by devices called oscillators. Musically, this alters the timbre or color of the sound. And what do we mean by timbre and color? Imagine you are listening to a small group play a composition, and at one point in the piece the guitar and the piano play the same note. Even though from the perspective of a wave-form we are hearing the same pitch and amplitude from the different instruments, it's the quality called timbre that distinguishes them. The "polyphonic" part of this synthesizer's name is much easier to define. The SubTractor can have up to 99 different voices playing simultaneously.

A Quick Pep Talk

Each component on this synth affects the wave-form and ultimately the sound. While it's very easy to feel bogged down by the physics of altering wave-forms, remember that the purpose of this section is to get a basic understanding of what each part of this synth does and then, using this knowledge, adjust these parameters until you've reached your ideal sound.

The SubTractor Interface

At first glance this sound module can look very imposing. All the dials and sliders and buttons make it seem more like a device you'd see in an airplane cockpit than something one might use to create music! Don't worry, it's not as overwhelming as it seems! Essentially, the SubTractor is broken down into three sections: the play parameters on the far left, the oscillators in the center and the filters on the right.

Play Parameters

All of the functions to the left of the grey vertical line on this synth can be described as the play parameters.

Patch

The very first thing we see in the upper left part of our interface beneath the name of this device is the Patch window. In red letters on black you'll see the words Init Patch. Patches are previously created settings, and they are available for almost every device in Reason 3.0. As well as taking advantage of preset patches, you can create your own patches and save them or adjust existing patches and re-save them as new patches. To the right of the Patch window are three buttons:

- **Select Previous/Next Patch** - When you load a patch into SubTractor, you can have access to the other patches in that folder and instantly load them using the up and down arrows to go to the previous or next patch respectively.

- **Browse Patch** - Clicking on this button will open the Patch Browser, which you can navigate to find preset patches or patches that you have saved.

- **Save Patch** - Clicking on this button will open the Patch Browser as well, and you can move to where you wish to save any patches you have created.

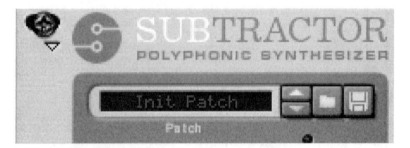

Loading a Patch

Let's examine some of the diverse sounds already created for the SubTractor Synth by loading a patch.

1. Click once on the Browse Patch button. It will open the Patch Browser window.

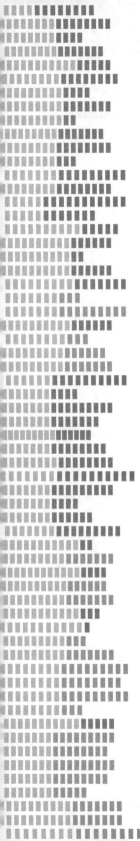

2. From the Locations part of the window, click on Reason
Factory Sound Bank.

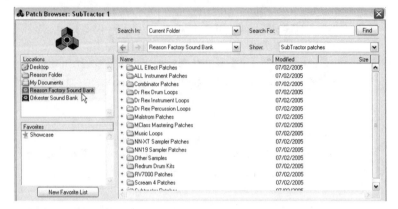

3. In the window on the right, scroll down and double click
SubTractor patches.

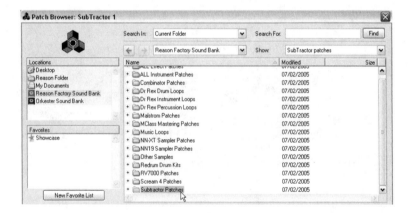

4. Now double click on PolySynths.

5. Double click on the first option called Accorditor.

You'll now be returned to the sound module.

Hit a few keys on your keyboard. Don't like what you're hearing? Try clicking once on the Select Next Patch button (the down arrow). Press a few keys on your keyboard. Try this with a few other patches to hear what they sound like.

Loading a Non-Synth Sounding Patch

Synthesizer and keyboard-type sounds are not the only kind that can be loaded into SubTractor. Let's try loading some of the others.

1. Click once on the Browse Patch button. It will open the Patch Browser window. (Notice that it defaults to your last selection.)

2. From the Locations part of the window, click on Reason Factory Sound Bank.

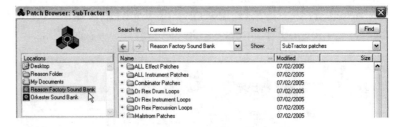

3. In the window on the right, scroll down and double click SubTractor patches.

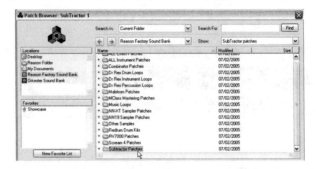

4. Choose from any of the selections (Bass, Fx, Pads, Percussion)

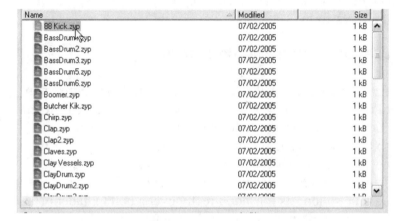

5. Double click on the first patch.

You'll now be returned to the sound module. Hit a few keys on your keyboard to listen to what that patch sounds like.

Use the Select Next Patch button to load and then listen to the other patches.

It's amazing to listen to the radical difference in sounds that can be created by one device simply by altering aspects of the wave-form!

(Re)initializing the Synthesizer

A time may come when you wish to return to the base setup of the SubTractor. Maybe you've been sampling the different patches available. Or perhaps you have experimented with so many knobs and buttons and sliders that all you hear is noise. You can easily return the synthesizer to its default setup by moving your pointer anywhere on the sound module so long as it is not directly over a button, fader or knob. Then right click your mouse button and select Initialize Patch.

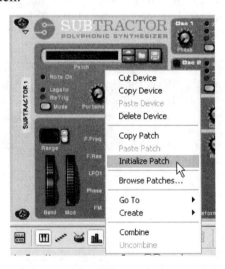

The Patch window will now indicate Init Patch, and all the settings will be at the default levels.

Low BW (bandwidth) On/Off Button

Selecting this button will remove some high frequency parts of the wave-form created by the sound module, most of which are rarely noticeable. The purpose is to ease the workload placed on your CPU. Clicking this button will illuminate the red light above it, indicating it is turned on.

Polyphony

Earlier we mentioned that SubTractor is a polyphonic synthesizer, meaning it can play many voices at the same time. Using the up and down arrows, you can define how many concurrent notes you allow the synth to play. Reducing the number to one means you are creating a monophonic patch. Why do this? As you've noticed from experimenting with patches, some sounds, such as drum or other percussion elements, are ideally played as notes.

Legato and Retrig Modes

Below the Patch window there is a button that allows you to select from two modes, Legato and Retrig.

Legato should be selected when you've set your Polyphony level to 1 (monophonic) while Retrig is best used when you're using multiple voices. Try this:

1. Set Polyphony to 1.

2. Click on the mode button to select Legato. Press and hold
down on a Keyboard key, then press another key.

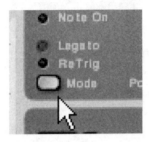

3. Click on the mode button again to select Retrig. Now
repeat the same action with the keyboard -- hold one key
down, then strike another.

Notice the difference? In Legato, when you strike the second
key, you hear the pitch change, but the envelope is not
restarted. There is no "attack" heard. In Retrig we hear the
full sound of the second key because the envelopes are
"retriggered" with full attack. The normal mode setting in
SubTractor is Retrig because we usually are using more than
one voice. If you are set to monophonic and want to create a
standout lead sound, you can select Legato.

Portamento

This small knob controls the timing of pitch change when
you go from playing one note to another. The effect is a
gliding or sliding from one pitch to the next. Turn this knob
all the way to the left for no portamento, all the way right for
the greatest effect.

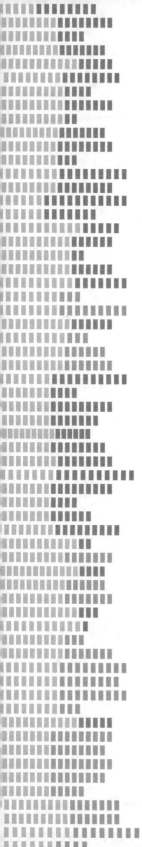

Ext. Mod (External Modulation Button)

Some MIDI keyboards have pedals, breath controllers or other add-ons that can give added expression to sounds being created. SubTractor can receive this MIDI controller data and manipulate it in one of four different parameters.

- **A. Touch (aftertouch or channel pressure)** - Most keyboards can send MIDI data that represent the force with which keys are pressed.

- **Expr (expression pedal)** - This takes the MIDI data sent by an expression pedal connected to your keyboard.

- **Breath (breath control)** - As you have heard by examining some of the many patches for SubTractor, some sounds are remarkable representations of wind instruments. With a breath control device attached to your keyboard, you can duplicate the envelope that would be created playing one of these instruments.

First you must select the type of external modulation you are bringing into the SubTractor. Then you can adjust the four parameters: F. Freq (filter frequency), LFO1 (low frequency oscillator 1), Amp (amplitude) and FM (frequency modulation) by turning their respective dials:

- To the left to decrease the value.

- Or to the right to increase the value.

Pitch Bend Wheel

Almost every MIDI keyboard has controls for pitch bend and modulation. These features are usually manipulated with a wheel. The wheels here perform the same function and will actually animate, duplicating your performance on the keyboard. In the event you don't have these wheels on your keyboard, or are not using a keyboard, you can effect wheels by clicking and holding, then dragging upward or downward. The Range button sets the pitch bend range. The highest range available is two octaves, represented by a value of 24.

1. Click the up/down arrows to select a range of 12.

2. Position your pointer over the Bend wheel and hold down the mouse button. Press a key on your keyboard. Drag upward with your mouse. The pitch is higher.

3. Drag downward with your mouse. The pitch is lower.

4. Click the up arrow to change the range value to 24.

5. Repeat instructions 3 and 4 to hear a greater range of pitch bend, both higher and lower.

Modulation Wheel

Similar to the external Modulation button, the Modulation wheel allows you to apply varying amounts of different parameters by dialing up or down. The elements we can affect with the Modulation wheel are:

- F. Freq (filter frequency)

- F. Res (filter resonance)

- LFO1 (Low Frequency Oscillator 1)

- Phase (offset)

- FM (frequency modulation)

Oscillators

The SubTractor synthesizer creates sound using oscillators -- devices that generate wave-forms. The two basic properties that an oscillator governs are frequency (or pitch) and wave-form shape. The wave-form type you choose to work with will determine the timbre of the final sound. As indicated earlier, we are in the world of waves, and by manipulating (or re-shaping) them we can create almost limitless sound variations. Just recall the difference in the types of sounds you heard when examining the patches, everything from piano-like and string sounds to percussion, wind instruments, fx and much more. SubTractor offers two oscillators, allowing you to combine wave-forms to create many new timbre possibilities. The center portion of the SubTractor interface contains the main oscillator elements:

- Osc 1 (Oscillator 1)

- Osc 2 (Oscillator 2)

- Noise (Generator)

- LFO 1 (Low Frequency Oscillator 1)

- Mod (envelope modulation)

- LFO 2 (Low Frequency Oscillator 2)

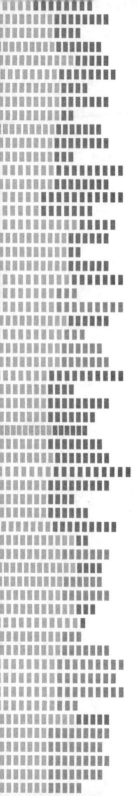

Oscillator 1

The first option in the top middle of the SubTractor interface is Oscillator 1, our main oscillator. The first illuminated box we can see is the Wave-form box. By clicking the up and down arrows (or click holding your mouse down and dragging upward or downward), you can scroll through the 32 wave-forms available to us. The first four options are basic and depicted by their actual shapes (Sawtooth, Square, Triangle and Sine). The next 28 choices are specialized wave-forms that provide the basic setup for many different-sounding instruments. Please refer to the Reason 3.0 Help menu for a description of the individual wave-form sounds. The next three boxes allow you to adjust:

- **Octave** - You can adjust this in steps from 0 to 9. The default setting is 4.

- **Semitone** - You can adjust the frequency in 12 semitone steps dividing one octave.

- **Cent** - This fine tuning field allows you to adjust in "cent" increments, which are 1/100th of a semitone (values range from -50 to +50).

Let's try listening to a few of the different waves and see what they sound like.

1. Click on the Mode button (just below and to the left of the Wave-form box) so that a red light is lit up next to the "o." (We'll describe exactly what Mode does shortly.)

2. Hold down any key on your keyboard. Click on the up arrow next to the Wave-form box and listen to the how your note changes as you cycle through different wave-form types.

3. Adjust the Octave, Semitone and Cent fields and listen to changes as you alter the frequency.

Beneath the Semi field is a red light/button called Kbd Track (keyboard tracking). When this button is lit, the pitch will change for every keyboard key you strike. When the button is unlit, the pitch of the oscillator will remain constant. This setting is used when you choose drum, percussion or fx sounds that need to remain the same pitch.

The Mode Button (phase offset modulation)

SubTractor gives you a unique way to take your selected wave-form and transform it into something much more complicated. What this feature does is to create a second, duplicate wave-form (within the same oscillator) whose phase you can offset. This phase offset effect can create exciting new timbres with various textures. Mode can be adjusted to one of three settings:

- "x" selects wave-form multiplication.

- "-" selects wave-form subtraction.

- "o" selects no modulation.

Once you have selected a mode, you can adjust the Phase knob to the left of this button to the desired amount of phase offset.

1. Select wave-form multiplication by clicking on the Mode button.

2. Press and hold a keyboard key while adjusting the Phase knob to hear how the timbre changes as you offset the wave-form phase. Try this with the subtraction method as well.

Oscillator 2

Oscillator 2 enables us to go from rich to richer - at least in the aspect of sound creation! Here we have a generator with all the options for creating a wave-form as Oscillator 1 -- including 32 wave-forms, octave, semitone and cent parameters, phase offset modulation and keyboard tracking. So how exactly do we get richer? Well, as seems to be the mantra of this chapter, it's all about the wave-form(s). By

creatively manipulating the interaction of the waves generated by both oscillators, fantastic new timbres will be born.

Mix

The Mix knob defines the amount of balance between the two oscillators. Turn the knob all the way to the left and you'll hear Oscillator 1 only. Turn it all the way to the right and, it will be Oscillator 2 alone. Set the knob at the twelve o'clock position to hear a balanced oscillator effect.

1. On Oscillator 1 turn the Phase Modulation off (the "o" setting).

2. Set the wave-form to Sawtooth (the default wave-form).

3. Set the Octave to 4 and leave Semi and Cent at 0.

4. Activate Oscillator 2 by clicking on the button next to Osc 2 so that it lights up red.

5. Set Oscillator 2's wave-form to Sine.

6. Press any key on your keyboard and then turn the Mix knob left and right to listen to the two wave-forms and how they blend.

FM (frequency modulation)

This is the term given when the frequency of one oscillator is modulated by the frequency of another. The oscillator whose frequency acts as the base sound is called the carrier, and the oscillator whose frequency does the modulation is called (appropriately enough) the modulator. For our purposes Oscillator 1 is the carrier, and Oscillator 2 is the modulator. The more we modulate the carrier (by increasing the amount of FM), the more we'll create a very electronic, almost staccato sound.

1. Leave the Oscillator settings the same as above but set the Mix knob at 12 o'clock.

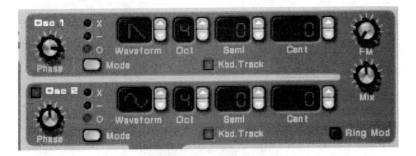

2. Play a few keys and while doing so rotate the FM knob its full range -- from all the way left to all the way right. The variations, you'll see, can be quite extreme.

3. Try to adjust the Octave, Semitone and Cent to fine tune the variations.

Ring Modulation

Underneath Oscillator 2's Cent window is a button called Ring Mod, which activates ring modulation.

What this does is multiply the Osc 1 and Osc 2 signals together, combining them to create a new signal of mixed frequencies. Selecting this button creates a timbre resembling the sounds of a bell.

1. Set the Osc 1 wave-form to a Square wave and the Octave to 4.

2. Turn on Osc 2 and set its wave-form to Sawtooth and the Octave to 4.

3. Play a chord on the keyboard. Now click on the button next to the Ring Mod button to turn it on. It will be red when turned on. Notice the change in the sound.

4. Increase the Osc 2 Semi value to 5. Toggle the Ring Mod button on and off to hear the changes.

Noise Generator

Some might think these dials generate hyperactive children. Actually, they don't. The noise generator generates... well, noise! You may be familiar with the term white noise, which is what the "snow" on an untuned television set sounds like. The noise generator is defaulted to work with Osc 2, but if you want to use it with Osc 1, you can deactivate Osc 2, then use the Frequency Modulation knob.

- **Decay** - This knob controls how fast the noise fades out after you hit a key. All the way to the left is the shortest amount of fade-out. Full right is the longest.

- **Color** - This knob controls the amount of tone (or character) in the noise. Rotate the knob to the left for lower pitched noise, to the right for higher pitched noise.

- **Level** - This controls the loudness of the noise. Left for less, right for more.

1. Click on the button next to Noise to activate it. It will light up red.

2. Make sure OSC 2 is deactivated.

3. Turn all the Noise knobs full to the right.

4. Press a key on the keyboard and rotate the FM knob from right to left to add noise. You're now hearing noise applied to OSC 1.

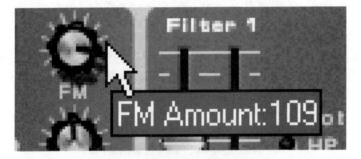

5. Activate OSC 2.

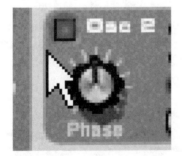

6. Turn the Mix knob all the way to the right and the FM knob all the way to the left. You're now hearing noise affecting OSC 2.

LFO 1 (Low Frequency Oscillator 1)

The LFO is an oscillator like OSC 1 and 2. However, its purpose in the SubTractor Synth is quite different. The first difference is that it can only generate low frequency wave-forms. The main difference, though, is that its job is to modulate the wave-forms created by the main oscillators, not to generate its own sounds. The quality that LFO can add to your patch is the audio effect of vibrato (the up and down changing of pitch).

LFO Sync

Clicking on this button and activating it (it will glow red) means you are choosing to synchronize the frequency generated by the LFO with the tempo you have defined in the Reason transport.

LFO Rate

This knob is the frequency generator of this oscillator. Turning the knob from left to right will adjust the frequency from lower to higher (slower to faster modulation). When the LFO Sync is activated, this knob will control the time division of the tempo.

LFO Amount

This knob determines how much vibrato you wish to add.

LFO 1 Wave-forms

The LFO offers six wave-forms (Triangle, Inverted Sawtooth, Sawtooth, Square, Random and Soft Random) that have varying modulating effects. Refer to the Reason help guide for specific descriptions of these parameters.

LFO 1 Dest (the Destinations button)

The LFO Dest button allows you to select:

- **Osc 1 & 2** - This LFO destination will modulate the pitch of both OSC 1 and OSC 2.

- **Osc 2** - This will modulate the pitch of Osc 2 only.

- **F. Freq** - This will modulate the filter frequency for Filter 1 (and for Filter 2 if they are linked).

- **FM** - When both oscillators are active, this will control the amount of frequency modulation.

- **Phase** - When the Phase Offset Modulation of Oscillators 1 & 2 is set to (x) or (-), meaning multiplication or subtraction, this will allow the LFO to control their phase.

- **Mix** - This LFO destination will control the mix.

LFO 2

SubTractor offers another Low Frequency Oscillator to add another layer of vibrato to your sound patch. LFO 2 does not have as many parameters as LFO 1 -- in particular, it does not give you the ability to choose a wave-form. But it has a few other features that are unique to it.

LFO 2 Dest

LFO 2 has half the destination options as version of LFO 1, offering Osc 1 & 2, Phase, and control of Filter Frequency 2. The destination parameter unique to LFO 2 is Amplitude, which controls the overall volume level.

LFO 2 Rate and Amount Knobs

These work in an identical fashion to the knobs in LFO 1, with the exception that you can't sync to temp.

LFO 2 Kbd (keyboard tracking)

When you have selected keyboard tracking on the main oscillators, turning this knob to the right will increase the frequency as you play higher notes on the keyboard.

LFO 2 Delay

Turning this dial to the right will increase the amount of time between when a note is played and when the LFO effect starts working.

Modulation Envelope

The Mod Envelope portion of the SubTractor synth enables you to control four envelope parameters (Attack, Decay, Sustain and Release) of a particular destination. Using these four sliders, you can control the amount of modulation over time. Just as with LFO 1, we can control the envelope of various destinations.

- **Osc 1** - This gives the mod envelope control of Osc 1's frequency.

- **Osc 2** - This controls Osc 2's pitch.

A Few Necessary Audio Terms

SubTractor has three envelope generators -- devices whose purpose is to control pitch, volume, frequency, modulation and more.

Envelope - The variance of an audio signal's intensity (or level) over time.

Attack - The time it takes for the envelope to be fully open (reach its full volume) when a note is generated. A high amount of attack means a slower effect (almost like a fade-in) while a lower value means the full volume level of a note is heard immediately.

Decay - The speed at which the envelope closes. (Again, a higher value means more of a fade-out effect. With a lower value the sound will cut out quickly.)

Sustain - The length of time a note is heard when a key is being held down.

Release - The length of time a note is heard after the key is released.

- **Osc Mix** - With both OSC 1 & 2 selected, this controls the modulation envelope of the oscillator mix.

- **FM** - Again with both oscillators selected, this controls the mod envelope of the frequency modulation.

- **Phase** - With both oscillators selected and Phase Offsets set to multiplication or subtraction, the mod envelope is controlled.

- **Freq 2** - This allows control of the mod envelope for Filter 2's frequency parameter.

Mod Envelope Invert Button

This button inverts the values of the Attack, Decay, Sustain and Release sliders.

Mod Envelope Amount

This knob allows you to select the degree of envelope modulation you wish to apply. Turn the dial all the way to the left for no effect and all the way to the right to fully apply all the envelope parameters.

Filters

As we have seen throughout this chapter, there are various ways of adjusting wave-forms to help to create different timbres. Filters assist in this process by isolating specific frequencies or ranges of frequencies and by filtering (or removing) them. An important term relating to filtration is the cut-off frequency. This is the point at which all the frequencies above (or below) are removed. SubTractor offers two filters as well as an element for controlling their envelopes.

Filter 1

SubTractor's main filter has sliders to alter frequency and resonance as well as a knob governing the filter keyboard track. By clicking the Type button, you can choose five types of filtration.

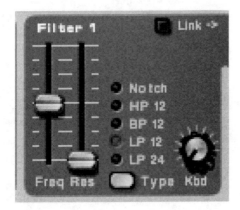

- **Notch** - This filter removes a narrow band of mid-range frequencies while leaving the higher and lower frequencies.

- **HP 12** - This "highpass" filter removes lower frequencies while leaving higher ones.

- **BP 12** - This is a "bandpass filter," the opposite of a notch filter, removing the high and low frequencies but leaving the mid-range.

- **LP 12** - This "lowpass" removes high frequencies and keeps low ones.

- **LP 24** - This is another type of lowpass filter.

Filter 1 Frequency

This slider defines the cut-off frequency. When it is set to its lowest value, only the lowest frequencies can be heard. When set to its highest value, all frequencies are heard. This parameter can also be controlled by the filter envelope.

Filter 1 Resonance

The resonance aspect of the filter works in collaboration with the Frequency slider. By adjusting the Resonance slider, we help emphasize the quality or character of the sound. This qualitative effect is better heard than explained, so let's listen to what it sounds like.

1. Click on the Browse Patch button.

2. Browse to the Reason Factory Sound Bank > SubTractor Patches > PolySynths > Balinese.

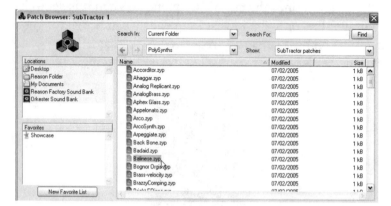

3. Note that the defaults for this patch have the Frequency slider at the midway point and the Resonance pulled all the way down. While tapping on a key on your keyboard, click and hold the mouse button and drag the Frequency slider up, then down, to listen to the effect of the cut-off point being changed. Return the slider to its midpoint.

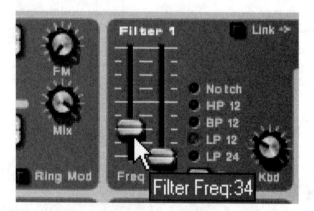

5. Leave the Frequency slider at this midpoint, then slide the Resonance slider up, then back down to its original position to hear the character change.

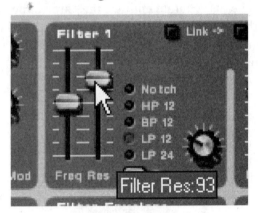

Filter 1 Keyboard Track

As with the other keyboard tracking options in SubTractor, turning this knob up will increase the frequency as you play progressively higher keys on the keyboard. Since the point of filters is to eliminate certain frequencies, you can lose a sound characteristic called "sparkle." If you feel the filter selected is removing sparkle, turn the Keyboard Track knob to the left (decreasing pitch change as you move up the keyboard) to compensate.

Filter 2

SubTractor's second offering is a single lowpass filter. While both filters act as separate entities, they are connected in series, with the signal passing through Filter 1 and then going to Filter 2. Let's see how the filters are used in conjunction.

1. Click on the Link button to the right of Filter 1 so it glows red (activated). Also, click on the red button between Link and Filter 2 so it is activated.

2. The default setting of Filter 2 for the Balinese is for the Filter slider to be at midpoint and the Resonance slider at zero. While tapping a key on the keyboard, pull Frequency to zero and Resonance to the midpoint and listen to the effect of a secondary filter being applied.

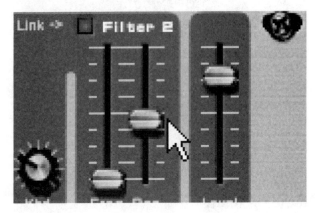

Filter Envelope

The Filter Envelope applies to options chosen on Filter 1 and has the same control options as the Mod Envelope (excepting the destination options). With this element of the SubTractor you are choosing how you would like to treat the envelope governing filter frequency over time.

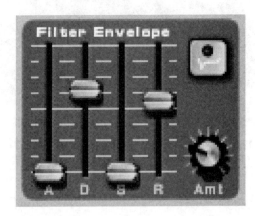

Amplitude Envelope

The Amplitude Envelope parameters affect how you control
the overall level characteristics in SubTractor.

SubTractor Velocity

Velocity has to do with how hard you strike notes on your
keyboard. While technically the velocity portion of the
SubTractor could be fall under the category of the Play
interface, since it's one of the last elements on the synth,
we'll discuss it now. There are nine knobs that control
velocity.

- **Amp** - This parameter controls the overall level based
  on how hard you strike keys. Turning this knob to the
  right (for a positive value) means the harder you strike
  a key, the louder the sound will be. Turning the knob
  to the left (for a negative value) means that no matter

how hard you strike a key, the volume will remain constant.

- **FM** - Rotating this knob to the right (for a positive value) will raise the amount of frequency modulation as you strike keys harder. Rotating the knob to the left (for a negative value) does the opposite.

- **M. Env** - Turning the knob to the right will increase the modulation envelope, and turning it to the left will decrease it the harder you strike keys.

- **Phase** - Again, based on how hard your strikes are, with a positive value you create more phase offset. With a negative value you create less.

- **Freq 2** - When this knob is turned positive, harder strikes will increase the frequency for Filter 2. In the negative position, this effect is inverted.

- **F. Env** - A positive value increases the amount of filter envelope while a negative value decreases it as you apply more key pressure.

- **F. Dec** - A positive value increases the amount of filter envelope decay while a negative value decreases it as you apply more key pressure.

- **Osc Mix** - The harder you strike the key (when the knob is turned right for a positive value), the greater the Oscillator 2 mix amount. Turning the knob to the left reverses this.

- **A. Attack** - When this amplitude envelope attack parameter control is positive, the harder you play, the more attack value you will have. Turning the knob to a negative position will invert this.

SubTractor Level

This fader controls the output level of the SubTractor Synth.

The Malström Graintable Synthesizer

Now that we've examined the SubTractor Synth in depth, the Malström's interface should not be intimidating. In fact, there are quite a few similarities between the two, including oscillators, filters and envelope and modulation tools. The primary difference is the method the Malström uses to generate sound. The SubTractor creates sounds by pure oscillation, using a process called subtractive synthesis.

The Malström works by morphing two methods of synthesis to create its own unique sounds. The first method is called "granular synthesis." It uses sampled sounds that have been subjected to complex processing, then sliced into tiny parts (from 5 to 100 milliseconds in duration) called "grains." Sounds are generated by applying variations to the grain properties and/or the manner in which they assembled. The resulting sound effects are called "graintables." The other aspect of Malström's sound creation is called "wavetable synthesis." This method is used to play back a periodic set of sampled wave-forms (called a wavetable). By combining these two methods, the synthesizer takes a graintable and treats it the same way it would a wavetable. The result, called "graintable synthesis," delivers a rich array of abstract sounds that can sound really incredible.

The Malström Play Parameters

The far left third of Malström's interface contains knobs and wheels that control parameters influencing how sounds are played. Here we see great similarity to the SubTractor:

- **Patch window** - Indicated in this window is the current patch loaded. As well you can scroll through loaded patches using the up/down arrows (select next/previous patch), and you can load and save patches.

- **polyphony** - As with the SubTractor synth, you can determine the number of voices you wish to play simultaneously – from monophonic to as many as 16 voices at one time.

- **legato** - Activated by an on/off button, this parameter allows you to control your sound as poly- or monophonic.

- **portamento** - Use this dial to change the amount of pitch between notes struck. Turn to the left for none, to the right for maximum pitch glide.

Malström Velocity

As with the previous synth, you can control various parameters affecting velocity -- the force with which keyboard keys are struck.

- **lvl: A (Level A)** - The volume control for Oscillator A. Turn to the right to increase, to the left to decrease.

- **lvl: B (Level B)** - Volume control for Oscillator B.

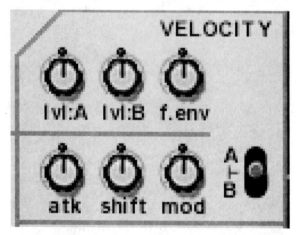

- **f.env (filter envelope)** - This overall velocity control is tied to the filter envelope parameters. Turn the knob to the right to increase the amount the harder you play notes, or to the left for the opposite.

- **A/B Selector Switch** - Tied to the next three knobs, this switch allows you to identify which synth elements you wish to engage -- Modulator/Oscillator A or B or both.

- **atk (attack)** - Turning the knob to the right will increase attack time. Turning it to the left will decrease attack time for Oscillator A or B or both.

- **shift** - This controls the shift parameter for Oscillator A or B, or for both.

- **mod (Modulation)** - By dialing right or left, you will increase or decrease the amount of modulation from Modulator A, B, or both.

Malström Pitch Bend & Modulation Wheels

Reason 3.0 accepts pitch and modulation wheel input from most MIDI keyboards. These parameters can also be controlled through the Malström interface.

- **Pitch Bend Wheel and Range** - Clicking and dragging this wheel up or down will change the pitch (up or down) with the amount determined by the value set in the range field (from zero to 24, representing a two-octave change).

- **A/B Selector Switch** - Directing which data are controlled by the next four knobs, this switch allows you choose between Modulator/Oscillator/Filter A, B or both.

- **index** - This parameter affects the modulation wheel's control of Oscillator A or B, or both. Turning the knob to the right will affect the active graintable's index position by moving it forward when the modulation wheel is dialed upward. Turning the knob to the left will move it backward.

- **shift** - This knob facilitates mod wheel control of the shift parameter of Oscillator A or B, or both.

- **filter** - Dialing this knob to the right will let the mod wheel raise the frequency when it is rolled upward. Dialing to the left means the frequency will decrease when the mod wheel is rolled upward.

- **mod** - This dial governs the total amount of modulation from Modulators A or B, or both. Turning it to the right will increase the modulation when the mod wheel is dialed upward, and turning it to the left means modulation will decrease as the wheel is dialed up.

The Malström Oscillators

The two oscillators built into Malström are found to the immediate right of the play parameters. They can generate pitch as well as play a graintable. With the minor exception of routing options, their parameter controls are identical.

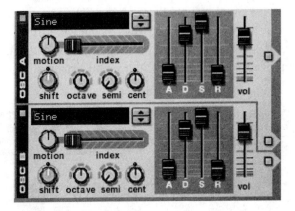

Oscillator On/Off Button

Located immediately above the label indicating the oscillator (A or B) is the on/off button. Clicking once on this will turn it yellow, activating it.

Oscillator Graintable Preset Window

The default graintable loaded is Sine Wave. This, however, is one of only 80 graintable presets we can choose! The graintables are divided into nine sound-type categories, including bass, Fx, guitars, miscellaneous instruments, percussion, synthesizers, voices, waves, and wind instruments. You can cycle through the list of presets by clicking on the up and down arrows to the right of the window, or you can click and hold your mouse button down in the window, which will reveal a menu listing all 80 presets.

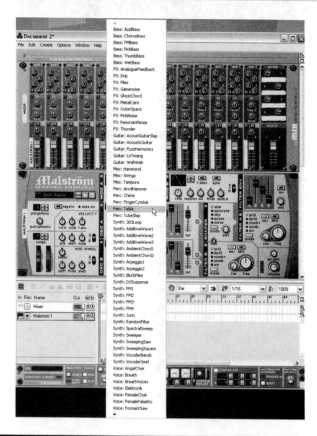

Oscillator Octave, Semitone and Cent Controls

These function in the same manner as their cousins in the SubTractor interface. The main exception is that the value is not shown in a window. To find out the value at which each is set, click/hold your pointer over the dial. The current value will be displayed.

Oscillator Amplitude Envelopes

Each oscillator has four sliders that let you to adjust the Attack, Decay, Sustain and Release envelope parameters the same way that you did with the SubTractor. In addition, there is a fader for controlling the oscillator's overall level.

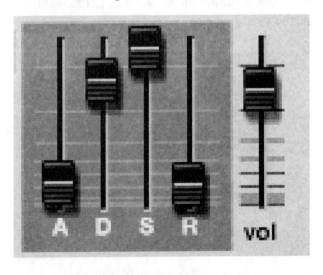

Oscillator Graintable Playback

Each Oscillator (A and B) has three parameters which control the playback of the graintable.

Index

Just over the Octave, Semi and Cent knobs is a horizontal slider called Index. It allows you to determine where graintable playback begins. The slider range is zero to 127.

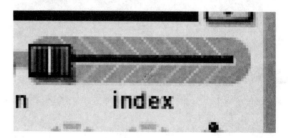

Motion

The yellow motion knob controls the playback speed of the graintable from one segment to the next. When the knob is rotated all the way to the left, there is no motion through the graintable and only the segment defined by the index slider will be played. Rotating the knob from left to right will increase the speed.

Shift

This blue knob shifts the pitch of the segment up or down (rotating left or right).

Oscillator Routing

Malström lets you send the signal generated by the oscillators through filters and other tools available through four buttons. We will discuss how the filters work with the oscillator's signal shortly.

- **Option A** - If this button is activated, the routing path will be Osc A > Shaper > Filter A > Output.

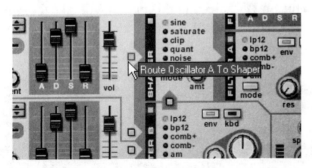

- **Option B** - If this button is activated, the routing path will be Osc A > Filter B > Output.

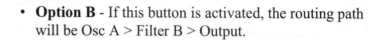

- **Option C** - Activating this button takes the signal from Osc B > Filter B > Output.

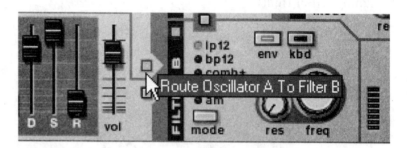

- **Option D** - Selecting this button will take the signal originating from Osc A or B, or both, and then route it or them through the Shaper > Filter A > Output.

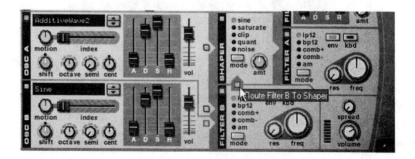

The Malström Modulators

At the center top of the interface are two Modulators (called A and B). These are also oscillators -- and specifically LFOs (low frequency oscillators). Just as with the SubTractor, their point is not to generate sounds but rather to use their wave-forms to modulate the sounds generated by Osc A and B, or by both. Some parameters are shared by the modulators:

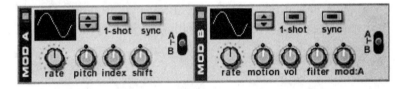

- **Curve** - By clicking the up/down arrows, you can cycle through 31 available wave-forms used to modulate the oscillators.

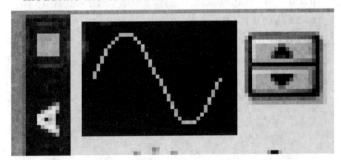

- **rate** - This yellow knob controls the frequency of the curve. Dial from left to right to go from a slow to fast modulation rate.

- **1 shot** - Activating this button tells the modulator to play the selected wave-form just one time.

- **sync** - Select this button to keep the modulation in time (synced) with the tempo of your song.

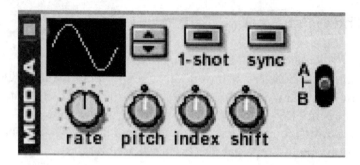

- **A/B Selector** - This feature allows you to apply that modulator's settings to Oscillator/Filter A or B or both.

Mod A

The first Malström modulator has three parameters that you can adjust to modulate the wave-form of the oscillators.

- **pitch** - You can adjust this knob to offset tone or pitch. Turn to the left for a lower sounding tone or to the right for a higher (brighter) tone. Keeping the knob in the 12 o'clock position means you do not wish to alter the pitch.

- **index** - Use this knob to adjust the offset of the index starting position.

- **shift** - The Shift knob will modulate the oscillator wave-form to affect the harmonic content.

- **mod B** - The second Malström modulator enables you to modulate the oscillators using four parameters from Mod A.

- **motion** - Turning this knob modulates the oscillators

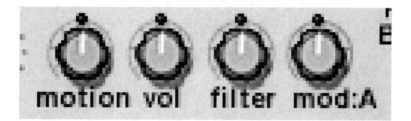

by changing their speed. Rotate left to slow down, right to speed up.

- **volume** - Lower (turn the knob left) or raise (turn the knob right) the level of the oscillators with this parameter.

- **filter** - With this knob you control the cut-off frequency for Filter A or B or both. Turn to the left for a lower cut-off frequency, to the right for higher.

- **mod A** - If you wish the change how much modulation is coming from Modulator A, use this knob. Turn to the left for less, or right for more.

The Malström Filters

Malström offers four filtration devices to help you further tweak the shape of your wave-form and ultimately mold the character of your sound creation. Although the interface is slightly different from that of the SubTractor, the way these filters work is quite similar. You can create a more diverse array of sounds using the Malström filters by using the different routing options described earlier.

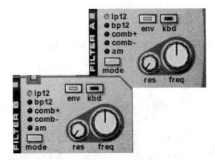

Filter A and B

Both filters have identical parameters to modify and shape sound character. Each has its own on/off button.

Mode

Just as with the SubTractor, you have a choice of which filter types -- in this case five options.

- **lp12** - A lowpass filter, this selection will cut out higher frequencies, leaving only the low ones.

- **bp12** - This bandpass filter lets a band of mid-range frequencies through while eliminating higher and lower frequencies.

- **comb + and comb** - This filter works by creating resonating peaks at certain frequencies. The effect is to create a series of delays with a very short delay time for each occurrence. The difference between a plus (+) comb filter and a minus (-) comb filter is the position of the peaks within the wave-form. In terms of what you will hear, the minus filter will cut out some lower frequencies.

- **am (amplitude modulation)** - This filter acts in the same way as the ring modulator on the SubTractor, taking two frequencies and multiplying them. In this case the filter takes a sine wave and then multiplies it with Osc A or B.

- **env (envelope)** - When lit, this button is tied to the filter envelope, which will modulate the cut-off frequency.

- **kbd (keyboard tracking)** - With this button clicked, the higher the keys you play on your keyboard, the higher the filter frequency will be. The lower the keys you play, the lower the frequency will be. If this button is not activated, the filter frequency is the same no matter what keys you play.

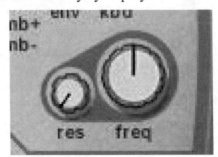

- **freq** - This knob is used to set the cut-off frequency of a particular filter. Dial the knob to the left for a lower cut-off or to the right for a higher cut-off. For the AM filter this will control the frequency generated by multiplied waves.

- **res** - Use this knob to control filter characteristics. With different filters you'll have different sound aspects. With the comb + or comb - filter, you can use the Resonance knob to control the amount of feedback created by the delays. With lowpass filters the more you turn the knob to the right, the more the frequencies around the set frequency will be emphasized. With the AM filter this knob controls the balance between the two multiplied wave-forms. All the way to the left is just the oscillator, and full right is the AM signal only.

Filter Envelope

This has the same parameter controls and functionality as the SubTractor filter envelope.

Shaper

The Malström Shaper is another tool for modifying the audio signal by altering the shape of the wave-form. The process is called "waveshaping synthesis." In some respects it can be considered a more advanced version of the SubTractor's noise tool. As with the all the other tools in the Malström, it is activated by clicking on its on/off button.

Mode

Depending on which mode you select, you can shape the wave-form to create a distinct sound character.

- **sine** - Choosing a sine wave creates a smooth, even sound.

- **saturate** - A rich, full sound is developed by saturating the original wave-form.

Malström Routing

Malström is not just a self-contained synthesizer. By using the audio inputs in the back of the device, you can route the audio signal from another device to take advantage Malström's filters. This is only one of the extras offered by Malström. Others include:

Sequencer Control - Hook up a pattern-controlled sound module (such as Matrix or ReDrum) to Malström to transfer note information.

- Gate Input - This lets pattern-controlled devices send Amp and Filter envelope control commands.

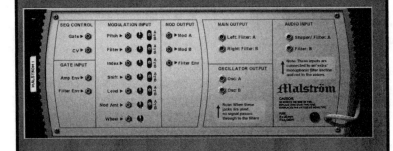

- Modulation Input/Output - Malström can accept any modulation output data from any other Reason device and then send them to another device.

- Audio Output - Malström can output directly from the oscillators, modulators or filters.

- **clip** - This mode "clips" sound for digital distortion.

- **quant** - Reducing the number of bits, this mode creates what can be described as a dirty, fuzzy noisy effect.

- **noise** - The original wave is multiplied with noise.

Amt (amount)

Dial the knob from left to right to go from no shaping to increasing the amount of shaping applied to the wave-form.

Volume and Spread

The last controls we can manipulate with Malström are volume and spread. Volume simply controls the overall output level. Spread controls the width of pan from the oscillators or filters. The greater the pan width, the more "distance" there will appear to be between the left and right channels. Turn the knob to the left for the least pan width, to the right for the most.

Device Central 6

By now you've started to build some serious momentum in terms of your understanding of Reason 3.0's devices. Understanding the basics of how the synthesizers work is an important launching point for your continued exploration of Reason and its array of creative devices. In this chapter we'll cover a wide range of topics from sampling and working with samplers to creating loops, building drum tracks and developing programs using pattern-based devices and sequencers. You'll learn about:

- **Sampling and the NN-19 Digital Sampler**

- **Editing Samples with the NN-XT Remote Editor**

- **Looping and the Dr:Rex Loop Player**

- **Building Drum Tracks with the Redrum Drum Computer**

- **Building Patterns with the Matrix Pattern Sequencer**

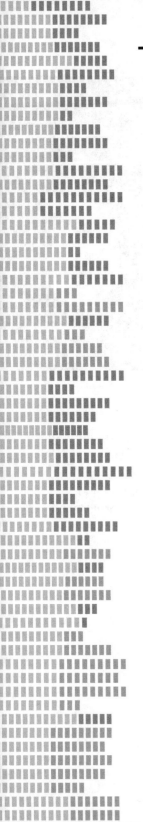

It's Time for Some Sampling

Unless you've somehow avoided listening to the radio for the past 20 years, you're quite likely to have experienced sampling. What started off as an essential component of rap and hip hop has now transcended almost every genre of popular music. Today sampling is everywhere. Part of the fun of listening to songs with samples is the game of trying to guess their origin and previous context. Reason 3.0 has powerful tools to enable you to create with samples. Before we explore that, let's start off with a very basic question… What exactly is sampling? Very simply, it's taking a pre-recorded sound (a sample) and playing it back. This could be the sound of an instrument playing a single note, a person speaking, a musical piece or, literally, anything that makes a sound.

The NN-19 Digital Sampler

The piece of real world hardware we call a sampler can both record and reproduce audio. The NN-19 can only play back samples, not record them. This does not, by any means, leave us without a plethora of options. The NN-19 comes with a wide variety of pre-made samples and patches, and if these are not enough, there are literally thousands of sources of samples available commercially, representing almost every kind of instrument or sound available. Should you wish to actually record your own samples, there are many multi-platform shareware and even freeware utilities for capturing and digitizing sounds via your computer's sound card.

Two Types of Sampling

The NN-19 offers both single and multi. Single sampling assigns a selected sample to the middle C key. This is known as the root key. Every other key struck higher and lower will have a change in pitch. The drawback is that the farther you move (higher or lower) on the keyboard away from the root key, the more processing the sample goes through (the greater the pitch change), and the more "unrealistic" it will sound. For this reason it is good to set up a key zone, which is a region of the keyboard surrounding the root key for playing a particular sample. We'll talk about key zones shortly. Multisampling offers much more authentic instrument sounds because each individual note has been sampled and then assigned to the appropriate key. The result is very realistic. Let's examine the difference between the two types of sampling.

1. Start with an empty rack. Right click your mouse and select Mixer 14:2 or choose it from the Create pull-down menu.

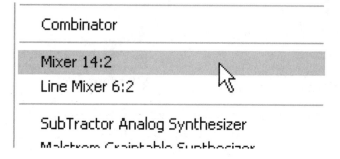

2. Now use one of the previous methods to create a new NN-19 Digital Sampler.

3. Click once on the Browse Sample button above the Key Zone window.

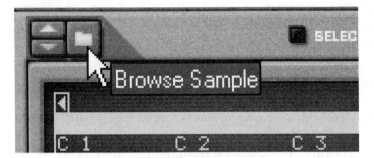

4. With the Sample Browser open select Reason Factory Sound Bank from Locations and browse to NN-19 Sampler Patches > Piano > GrandPiano > PianoC3_4x.wav.

5. If you wish to audition this sample from the Sample Browser window, you can, then click OK.

6. Notice that the sample loaded into the NN-19 Key Zone window.

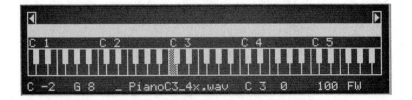

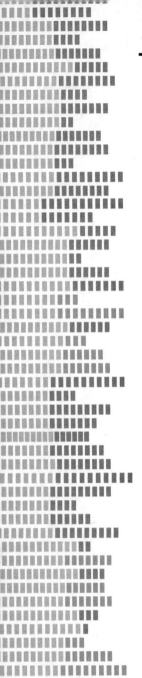

7. Press the middle C on your keyboard. It should sound just like a grand piano's C. Now go up a full octave key by key till you hit the next C. The higher you go, the more the pitch changes, the more "artificial" or processed the grand piano sample sounds.

Now let's listen to a multi-sampled example.

1. Right click anywhere on the NN-19 that isn't a button or dial and select Initialize Patch. You can also select this from the Edit menu.

2. Click on the Browse Patch button.

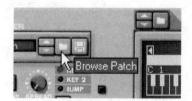

3. With the Patch Browser open select Reason Factory Sound Bank from Locations and browse to NN-19 Sampler Patches > Piano > GRANDPIANO.smp.

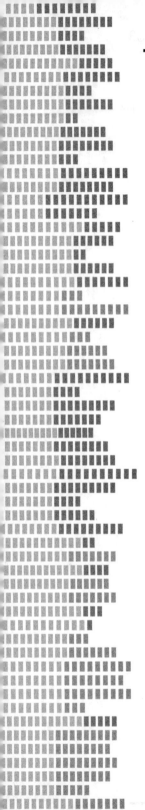

4. Play the same notes as you did in the previous example. Notice the much more realistic sound as you play higher and lower.

Loading File Types

While using the Browse Sample button allows us to load a single sample, when we load a patch, we are actually loading a number of samples at the same time. The NN-19 can load a variety of standard file types (at any sample rate or bit depth) to be used as samples.

- *Wave (.wav)*

- *AIFF (.aif)*

- *SoundFonts (.sf2)*

- *REX slices and files (.rex, .rcy, .rex2)*

- *Sample Patch Format (.smp) - Sample patches are saved as this file type and are composed in multiple .wav or .aif files.*

The point of our previous exercise was not to diminish the idea of using single samples. Largely, when we choose to use the NN-19, we don't necessarily want to duplicate an instrument sound. We usually want to start with that sound and then build on it to create something very unique.

Key Zones

As mentioned earlier, key zones are areas of keys on the keyboard that you designate to play a certain sample. There are a couple of straightforward methods to choose from. As we go through these exercises, you'll also learn how some of the knobs on the NN-19 operate.

Setting up a Key Zone - Method 1

1. Start with clean slate. Right click anywhere on the NN-19 that isn't a button or dial and select Initialize Patch. You can also select this from the Edit menu.

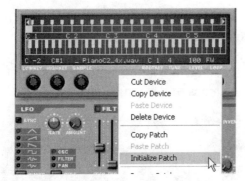

2. Click once on the Browse Sample button above the Key Zone window. Alternately, you can right click on the window and select Browse Samples from the menu that appears.

3. With the Sample Browser open select Reason Factory Sound Bank from Locations and browse to NN-19 Sampler Patches > Bass > SlapBass > ThumbC2,High.wav

4. If you wish, audition this sample from the Sample Browser window, then press the Play button.

5. Click OK. The file name appears in the Key Zone window underneath the keyboard. Note that the entire region above the keyboard is highlighted, meaning that all keyboard keys will play this sample.

6. Holding the ALT key down, click once above the C2 key, then once above the C4 key. A two-octave region appears highlighted above the keyboard, bordered by two handles. You can click, hold and use your pointer to drag the handles to ensure that they are exactly where you want them.

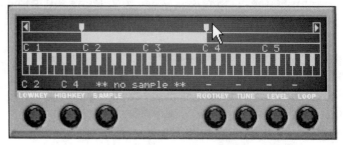

7. You may also use the two knobs called Low Key and High Key to move your lower and upper handles respectively. While the handles show you visually on the keyboard where you are, above the low and high key knobs you'll see the names of the actual keys.

8. Play the keys in the two-octave range between the C's on your keyboard. Now try to play outside this range. You hear only the keys that are isolated by the key zone.

Previewing

Hold down the Alt key and move your pointer over the keyboard. The icon will change to a plus sign and a speaker. Click on a key to preview.

Setting up a Key Zone - Method 2

1. Clear the slate again by choosing Initialize Patch from the Edit menu or from the menu that appears by right clicking on the Key Zone window.

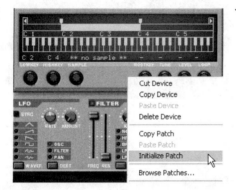

2. From either of the same menus from the previous instruction, select Split Key Zone. Now the region above the keyboard shows one handle with one side key zone highlighted.

3. Repeat instruction 2. We see that the highlighted key zone is gone, and still we see only one handle.

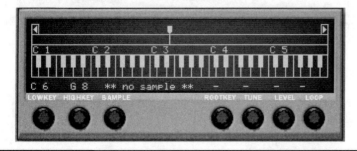

4. Click on the scroll arrow at the top right of the Key Zone window a few times. The keyboard will scroll over to reveal a second handle and a highlighted region to the right of it.

5. Click on the handle on the right side and drag it so that it is above C4. Notice that the selected key zone grows larger.

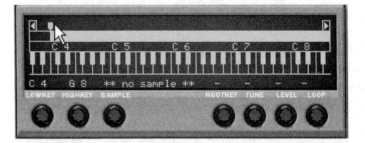

6. Click on the scroll arrow at the top left of the Key Zone window a few times until you can see the previous handle and the C2 key.

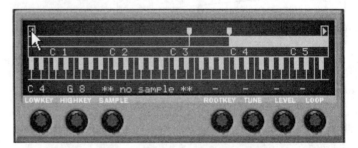

7. Click, hold and drag the left handle so that it's over C2.

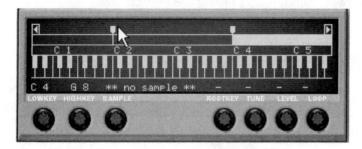

8. Click once in the region between the two handles (between C2 and C4). It now becomes highlighted.

9. Click once on the Browse Sample button above the Key Zone window or right click on the window and select Browse Samples from the menu that appears.

10. With the Sample Browser open select Reason Factory Sound Bank from Locations and browse to NN-19 Sampler Patches > Bass > SlapBass > ThumbC2,High.wav

11. If you wish, audition this sample from the Sample Browser window, then press the Play button.

12. Click OK. The file name appears in the Keyboard window underneath the keyboard.

13. Play the keys in the two-octave range between the C's on your keyboard. Now try to play outside this range. You hear only the keys that are isolated by the key zone.

I'm sure that you noticed we learned a few more things in the alternate method than in the first method. Let's recap. In addition to learning how to create a key zone, we also learned how to move key zone handles with the pointer and, with the low key and high key knobs, scroll through the full length of the keyboard and select a key zone. Key zones cannot overlap.

Loading a Second Sample

The beauty of working with single samples and key zones is that we can assign multiple samples across the keyboard. To show how this works, we'll continue from where we were in the last example.

1. Click on the key zone to the right of the one we were using previously to select it. Notice now that under the keyboard it says, **no sample**.

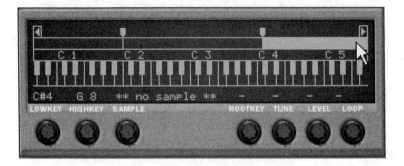

2. Click once on the Browse Sample button above the Key Zone window. Or you can right click on the window and select Browse Samples from the menu that appears.

3. With the Sample Browser open select Reason Factory Sound Bank from Locations and browse to NN-19 Sampler Patches > Synth and Keyboard > MelStrings > MelS C5.wav

4. If you wish, audition this sample from the Sample Browser window, then press the Play button.

5. Click OK. The file name appears in the Key Zone window underneath the keyboard.

6. Select the previous key zone by positioning your mouse between the handles and clicking once. Notice that the ThumbC2,High sample is listed there. Now play across the keyboard keys, playing higher. Notice that your keyboard is now split into key zones and will play the bass sample across one set of keys and the synth across the higher keys.

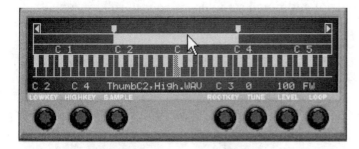

Solo Sampling

When you have more than one sample loaded but wish to hear what a single one will sound like across the length of the keyboard, activate the Solo Sample button at the top of the interface. Select the key zone, then this button, and you will hear that key zone's sample on every key of the keyboard. This will work if the "Select Key Zone via MIDI" button is turned off.

Using Key Zones with Multiple Loaded Samples

The methods we have just described for loading samples into key zones create assigned samples. (The samples are essentially "assigned" to a single or multiple key zones.) As you go through the process of loading and arranging your multiple samples, you will likely end up with some unassigned samples or samples that are not associated with a particular key zone. Even though unassigned, these samples have not disappeared. Whenever we load a sample into the NN-19, it resides in the sample memory, which can store numerous samples. We can access them as needed. We'll build from our previous example and start by loading a couple of additional samples into our third key zone.

1. Click once to select the third key zone. It will say **no sample** at the bottom of the Keyboard window.

2. Click once on the Browse Sample button above the Key Zone window. Or you can right click on the window and select Browse Samples from the menu that appears.

3. With the Sample Browser open select Reason Factory Sound Bank from Locations and browse to NN-19 Sampler Patches > Strings > Cello > C2_1.wav

4. If you wish, audition this sample from the Sample Browser window, then press the Play button.

5. Press OK. The file name of the sample appears in the Key Zone window just underneath the keyboard. You have loaded the third key zone with the cello sample.

6. Click hold over the Select Sample knob and slowly drag upward. Notice the name of the sample changing as it cycles through all the samples currently in memory. Rotate the knob through all three samples until you reach the fourth option, which is **no sample**.

Very Important Key Zone Information

Even though we have assigned specific samples to specific key zones, using the Sample knob, we can apply any loaded sample to a selected key zone!

7. Repeat instructions 2-5, but this time load the sample found at NN-19 Sampler Patches > Mallet and Ethnic > Kalimba > Kal2A21.wav.

8. Using the Sample knob, cycle through the four sample choices you now have. Try pressing a few keys on your keyboard (from this selected key zone) while using the Sample knob to move through the loaded samples list. You will hear all four different samples!

So what did we just learn? That we can have more samples loaded than we have key zones and can also re-arrange them quickly and easily.

Key Zone Selection Alternative

Another way to select a key zone is by activating the Select Key Zone via MIDI button. When you play a key on the keyboard, it will automatically select the key zone in whose range it falls.

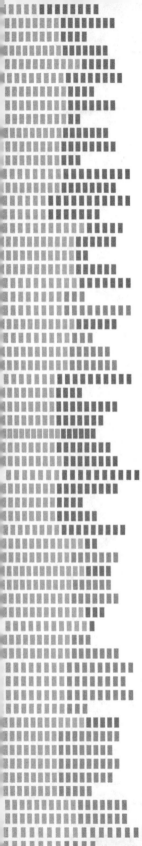

Zone Map and Saving Patches

When we loaded a patch earlier, we actually loaded a group
of individual samples represented by the patch. In the
keyboard window these samples are represented by a number
of key zones. Together all the key zones on one keyboard are
called a Zone Map, which can be saved as a patch. When we
save a patch, we are also saving the loaded samples
(including the unassigned ones). Let's take a moment to save
all the key zones we just built.

1. Click on the Save Patch icon.

2. Browse to the location you wish to save. Name your patch
appropriately and click on save.

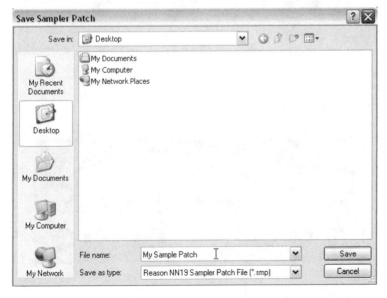

Let's take a moment to reload our patch and see if all the samples are still there.

1. Select Inialize Patch from the Edit menu or by right clicking on the key zone window.

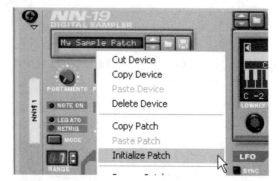

2. Click the Browse Patch button to load the patch.

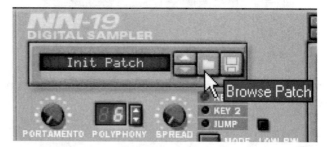

3. Browse and find your patch and double click on it. It will now be loaded.

4. Click on a key zone to select it.

5. Use the Sample knob to cycle through all the samples. All of them will be there, even the unassigned one.

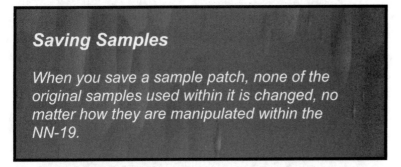

Saving Samples

When you save a sample patch, none of the original samples used within it is changed, no matter how they are manipulated within the NN-19.

Deleting Unused Samples

During the course of your experimentation, you'll create the perfect zone map with all the right sounds. However, since you loaded so many samples, you may end up with some unassigned ones that are no longer necessary.

1. Select the key zone on the far left.

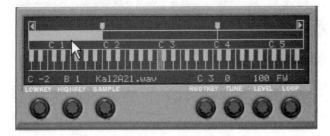

2. Turn the Sample knob so that it reads Kal2A21.

3. Select the key zone in the center.

4. Turn the Sample knob so that it reads ThumbC2,High.

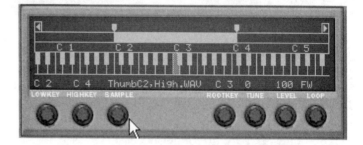

5. Select the key zone on the far right.

6. Turn the Sample knob so that it reads MelS_C5.

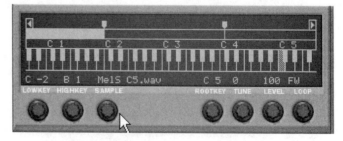

7. Right click on the Key Zone window to bring up the menu and select Delete Unused Samples.

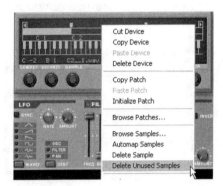

8. Select any key zone.

9. Use the Sample knob to dial through the available samples. Note that the three previous samples are there, but not C2_1, the cello sample. It has been deleted.

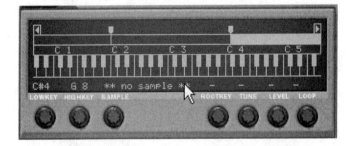

Root Key

The root key represents the assumed true note pitch for the sample. For example, if you loaded a sample of a flute playing D sharp, you would want to ensure that the root key assigned on the keyboard was D sharp. That way, all the other keys on the keyboard surrounding it would be in proper tune. On the keyboard in the NN-19, the root key is displayed as a "greyed out" key.

1. Use one of the methods learned earlier to Initialize Patch.

2. Use one of the methods you learned previously to load a sample.

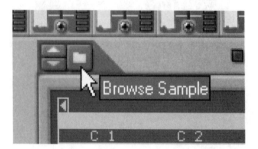

3. Browse to NN-19 Sampler Patches > Brass and woodwind > Flute > and load FltD#3.wav by double clicking on it or selecting it and pressing the OK button.

4. It defaults our root key to be set at C3 on our keyboard. Click hold your pointer on the Root Key knob and drag upward slowly until the key value about it reads D#3. Now the root key is properly set.

Creative Root Key

When using non-instrument samples, the regular purpose of a root key may not always apply. A sample of a person speaking or a percussion or sound effect is not necessarily tied to a particular note, but the creative placement of a root key could achieve some interesting results.

Tune Knob

As you build your key map by adding samples and creating key zones, you may find that they are not in tune with each other, particularly if they come from different sources. By adjusting the Tune knob to the left, you will lower the pitch of a key zone, and by turning it to the right you will raise the pitch.

Level Knob

Use this knob to lower (dial left) or raise (dial right) the volume of a specific key zone.

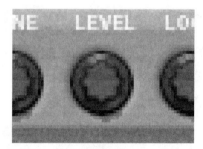

Loop Knob

Most samples are fairly short. To hear them for a longer time (for example, when you're holding down a keyboard key), you need to loop them. Most samples created in a sample editor have a loop start and end point that are designed for the most seamless-sounding loop. Samples without these prescribed loop start/end points will loop from the actual beginning to end. While this parameter is offered as a knob, it really acts as a switch with three settings.

- **Off** - This setting will play the sample for its actual duration and not loop it.

- **FW** - This loops the sample by playing from loop start point to finish point, then returning to the start point to begin again.

- **FW-BW** - This plays the sample from the loop start to finish, then plays it backward from finish to start, then continues from the start again.

Automapping Samples

The NN-19 has a quick way of automatically arranging samples into key zones based on the locations of their root keys.

1. Use one of the methods learned earlier to Initialize Patch.

2. Use a previously learned method to Browse Sample and shift-click to select a group of samples, then click OK to load them.

3. Rotate the Sample knob while looking at the sample name in the Key Zone window. Even though there are no key zones set up, you will cycle through the names of the samples you loaded.

4. Right click on the Key Zone window to reveal the pull-down menu and select Automap Samples or choose this option from the Edit menu.

5. A group of key zones is created for all the samples based on their root keys.

The NN-19 Play and Synth Parameters

If we browse quickly through the rest of the NN-19 interface, it seems that we're in familiar territory. Since we've covered these in depth in the previous chapter, we won't repeat ourselves here. One important thing to note... All the play and synth parameters we adjust here affect the entire patch, not individual samples or key zones.

The NN-XT Advanced Sampler and Remote Editor

The NN-XT is a device split into two sections: the main panel and the remote editor. Like the NN-19's play and synth controls, the main panel controls parameters that affect an entire patch. The remote editor works similarly to the Key Zone window (and its controls) but offers a much wider array of tools including:

- **Advanced Key Map Control** - You can adjust settings for individual samples.

- **Layered Samples** - You can overlap samples and key zones across the same keyboard key range.

- **Additional Sample Types** - You can import SoundFont presets and samples.

- **Expanded Output** - You can route samples to up to eight stereo outputs so they can be affected individually.

- **Velocity Control** - You can lock samples to play above specific velocity ranges, activate key maps by velocity and crossfade with velocity.

Adding an NN-XT to the Rack

1. Right click in the empty rack area and select NN-XT Advanced Sampler from the menu or choose it from the Create menu.

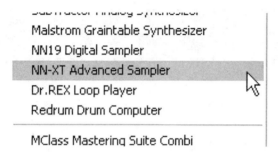

Malstrom Graintable Synthesizer

NN19 Digital Sampler

NN-XT Advanced Sampler

Dr.REX Loop Player

Redrum Drum Computer

MClass Mastering Suite Combi

2. The NN-XT will appear in the rack. The remote editor is minimized, so reveal it by clicking once on the right-pointing arrow.

The NN-XT Main Panel

Across the NN-XT's main panel interface you'll notice a quite a few tools that will be familiar from our examination of the synthesizers.

- Pitch Bend Wheel

- Modulation Wheel

- External Control

- High Quality Interpolation

- Save/Load Patch

- Filter

- Amplitude Envelope

- Modulation Envelope

- Master Volume

These wheels and knobs control the parameters affecting the entire patch. Please refer to the previous chapter for the specifics of how each function works.

The NN-XT Remote Editor

The most unique feature of the NN-XT, compared to the NN-19, is its ability to modify individual sample settings. Since it is an editor, it has useful tools to accomplish this.

Working with Samples

Across the bottom of the Key Map display you will see the Sample Parameters that allow you to adjust various aspects controlling the samples. We'll cover parameters unique to the NN-XT.

- **Start and End Knobs** - This is the first group of sample-editing knobs. With them we can indicate where we wish the sample to start and end playing.

- **Loop Start and End Knobs** - Depending on the nature of the sample, we may not necessarily wish it to loop from its natural beginning to end. With these knobs we can isolate the region that gives us the most seamless sound.

- **Play Mode** - As with the editor version of the Loop knob from the NN-19, there are five loop modes available here.

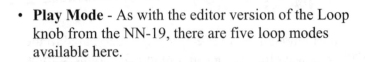

Frames

The start and end points are given in percentages representing the entire length of the original sample. The units the editor works in are called "frames," which are simply increments making up a sample.

- **FW** - The sample will play once and not repeat.

- **FW-Loop** - The sample will play once all the way through, then jump back to the start point and continue to the end, repeating infinitely.

- **FW-BW** - The sample plays from beginning to end, then plays from end to beginning and repeats.

- **FW-SUS** - The sample plays in the FW-Loop mode for as long as you hold down the keyboard key. When you release the key, the sample will play to its actual end point (not the loop end point).

- **BW** - The sample will play from the end to the start point once, without looping.

- **Lo and Hi Velocity Knobs** - Unlike the NN-19, with this editor you can actually overlap key zones. By using these knobs you establish which zones (samples) are played on the keyboard based on how hard you strike the keys. You can let each sample play across the full velocity or a specific range of velocities. You can even overlap values to trigger multiple samples based on velocity.

Velocity Range

When you change the velocity range (so that it's less than the full 0-127 range), your sample velocity range in the Key Map display will be shaded with diagonal lines.

- **Fade In and Fade Out Knobs** - Using these controls, you can create a fantastic and subtle transition between overlapping samples using crossfades.

Overlapping and Crossfading Key Zones in the NN-XT Editor

1. Let's start by loading the NN-19 sample patch we created earlier. Click on the Browse Patch icon in the NN-XT main panel. Browse to where you saved it and use the methods described earlier to load it.

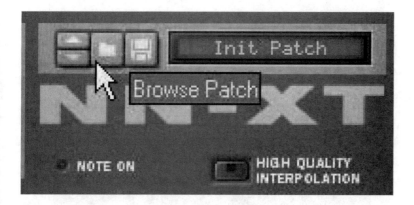

2. Click on the middle sample listed in the Sample column of the Key Map display (ThumbC2,High.wav). This will select that sample.

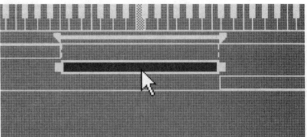

3. Grab the right handle and drag it to the right by a few notes. It will now overlap the sample immediately beneath it (MelS_C5.wav)

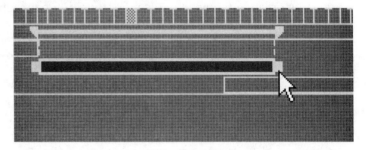

4. On your keyboard play the region of overlapping keys. You'll hear both samples paying simultaneously.

5. If it is not already selected, select the middle sample (ThumbC2,High.wav) by clicking on it.

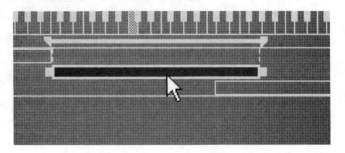

6. Rotate the Fade Out knob so it reads 50.

7. Select the bottom sample (MelS_C5.wav) by clicking on it.

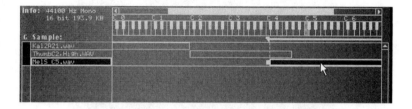

8. Turn the Fade In Knob to 100.

9. Now play the keys again and notice the smoother transition, with the samples fading in and out.

- **Alt Knob** - You can select on or off with this knob. When you turn it on, it activates an algorithm for alternating between zones during playback. The effect is a naturalistic switchover with no repetition.

- **Out Knob** - With this you can choose one of eight stereo output pairs and in this way have separate outputs for this many stereo zones, which you can then route (from the back of the NN-XT) to the mixer, effects devices, etc.

Group Parameters

You can select multiple zones by shift clicking them. Mulitple selected zones can have their certain values adjusted globally, as they are treated as a group. In the upper left hand portion of the NN-XT's remote editor you will see Group Parameters, where you can modify:

- Key Polyphony

- Legato/Retrig

- LFO Rate

- Portamento

Synthesizer Parameters

Forming an L shape across the bottom left portion of the
remote editor are parameters we have seen before in our
examination of the synthesizers. These are:

- Modulation

- Velocity

- LFO 1 and 2

- Modulation Envelope

- Pitch

- Filter

- Amplitude Envelope

If you examine the modulation parameters, you'll notice two small buttons underneath each dial, one marked with a W, the other with an X. Activating W will give the Modulation wheel control of that dial's parameters. Selecting X means the External Control wheel will govern those parameters.

The Dr:Rex Loop Player

There's nothing like a little repetition to make a good song great. Part of what has taken electronic music to the next level in terms of innovation is the creative application and modification of loops. Loops are just what they sound like: repeated groups of sounds arranged in such a way as to be compelling and addictive to the ears. The Dr:Rex loop player is different from other devices we have examined in that it doesn't load or save patches. There are three file types that can be loaded:

- .rex - REX files

- .rcy - RCY files

- .rex2 or .rx2 - REX S files

These files are created in a Propellerhead program called ReCycle, which allows you go create loops. As its name states, Dr:Rex is a loop player, not an editor. Truthfully, though, Dr:Rex is much more than a player because it enables us to modify a number of parameters. In addition, we can do some editing on the pre-made loop once it has been placed in the sequencer.

REX Slices

The base unit we work with in Dr:Rex is the slice. In ReCycle the loop is cut into small incremental pieces. Within Dr:Rex we can work with these "slices" to customize the sound of loops.

Creating a Dr:Rex Loop Player, Loading, then Playing a Loop

1. Starting with an empty rack, right click your mouse and select Mixer 14:2 or choose it from the Create pull-down menu.

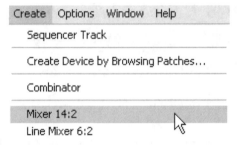

2. Right click in the rack and select Dr.Rex Loop Player or choose it from the Create pull-down menu.

3. Click on the Browse Loop button (the button with the folder icon) to load a loop.

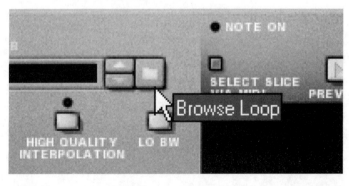

4. Using the Loop Browser, select Reason Factory Sound Bank from Locations and browse to Dr Rex Drum Loops > Drum N Bass > Drb27_Krispy_150_eLAB.rx2.

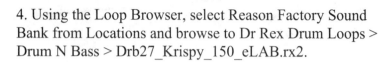
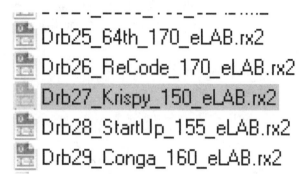

5. Press the Preview button above the Waveform display to hear the loop. Press it again to stop.

Synthesizer Controls

As with so many devices we have examined, the Dr:Rex allows synthesizer parameters to modify the loop. Here we can manipulate:

- Polyphony

- Range

- Pitch Bend Wheel

- Modulation Wheel

- Velocity

- Oscillator Pitch

- Filter

- LFO

- Filter Envelope

- Amplitude Envelope

Slice Controls

Along the bottom of the Waveform display are six knobs with which we can modify slices making up the loop.

- **Transpose** - Turning this knob left or right changes the key that the loop is in. This is visually indicated on the keyboard represented in the Waveform display.

- **Slice** - Turning this dial lets you select any slice in the loop. A selected slice will have a background made up of red dots instead of a black background.

Slicing Options

You can also choose a slice by clicking on it with the cursor. Above the Waveform display is a button called Select Slice via MIDI. When you click on this, it will let you select a slice based on a key representing it on the keyboard. (Slices are mapped to the keyboard in consecutive semi-tone increments). When this button is activated and you press the Preview button, the slice will be indicated as it plays.

Pitch - This lets you change the key a slice is in.

Pan - This gives you left-right pan capability depending on how you turn the knob.

Level - This sets slice volume.

Decay - This reduces the length of individual slices.

You can listen to a slice by holding down the ALT key (the cursor will change to a plus sign and speaker icon) and clicking on the slice in the Waveform display.

Copying the Loop to the Sequencer

1. In the timeline, move the left and right locators to isolate the region in which you'd like the loop to appear.

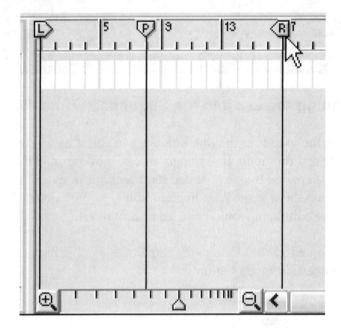

2. Press the To Track button above the Waveform display or right click anywhere on Dr:Rex and choose Copy REX Loop to Track.

Editing the Loop in the Sequencer Timeline

Once the loop is in the timeline, we can edit it using Arrange mode or Edit mode. In Arrange we can move around the groups created by the repeated loop sections or even ungroup them to move individual notes. A more detailed way to edit them would be to go to Edit mode.

1. Toggle to Edit Mode in the sequencer by clicking on the Arrange/Edit mode button.

2. Activate the Key, Rex and Velocity lanes by clicking on their buttons.

3. Expand the timeline and zoom in to see the lanes as large as possible.

Now you could choose the selection tool and move around, re-arrange or delete individual slices, or change velocity levels. Also, if you recorded some automation, you could activate that lane and manipulate the different parameters that were automated.

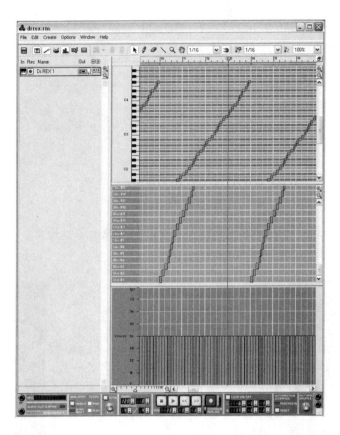

The Redrum Drum Computer

The deep dark secret that everyone keeps well hidden is this: we all want to be the drummer. Reason 3.0 allows us to fulfill that fantasy with the Redrum drum computer. This device is a little different from the others we've seen so far because it falls into the category of "pattern devices." These work by using a built-in sequencer to play back a pattern of a certain length. Some of these devices have a sound source (like the Redrum) while others (such as the Matrix Pattern Sequencer) need sounds generated by an external source. Before we examine the Redrum interface, let's start by loading the Remix mixer and then the Redrum.

1. Right click in the empty rack and select Mixer 14:2 to create a mixer.

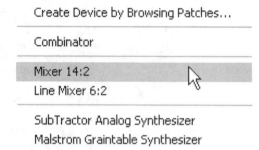

Create Device by Browsing Patches...

Combinator

Mixer 14:2

Line Mixer 6:2

SubTractor Analog Synthesizer

Malstrom Graintable Synthesizer

2. Right click in the empty part of the rack and select Redrum Drum Computer.

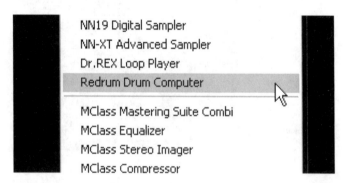

NN19 Digital Sampler

NN-XT Advanced Sampler

Dr.REX Loop Player

Redrum Drum Computer

MClass Mastering Suite Combi

MClass Equalizer

MClass Stereo Imager

MClass Compressor

The Redrum will automatically be patched to the Remix's Channel 1 stereo inputs.

Global Redrum Settings

These are found along the far lower left hand side of the Redrum.

Master Level

At the top left is the Master Level control, which determines the overall volume of the output from this device.

Patch Select

By now we're quite familiar with loading, saving and moving the arrows up and down to select a patch. Let's load a patch to start.

1. Click on the Browse Patch button.

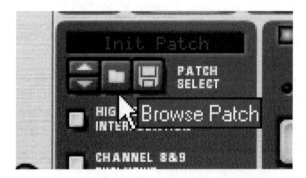

2. From the Reason Factory Sound Bank browse to Redrum Drum Kits > Heavy Kits > and load DublabHeavyKit3.drp by double clicking on it or selecting it and pressing the OK button.

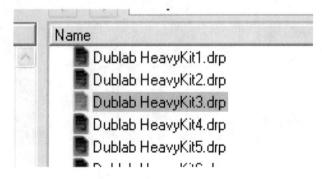

The sample name will be visible in red in the window above Patch Select, and if you look above all the drum channels, you'll see that individual samples are loaded in each one.

High Quality Interpolation

As with our synths and other devices, turning this feature on will improve the audio quality of our sample playback. It also means more processor power is being used, so keep your eyes on the CPU meter on the Reason transport. If it's showing heavy usage and you've got a lot of devices and effects working together, turn this off to conserve power.

Channel 8 & 9 Exclusive

Some samples used in the drum kit -- the sound of high hat cymbals, for example -- are tied together. By selecting this button, you are telling Redrum that when one sound (such as the open part of the high hat) is being played by channel 8, it should be cut off immediately when channel 9 (the closed part of the high hat) is activated. This also works reversed when this button is selected so that when channel 8 is played, 9 will be deactivated. If the samples loaded to channels 8 and 9 are not linked, deselect this button.

Drum Channels

Taking up the top three quarters of the Redrum interface are the drum channels. At first glance they bear a close resemblance to the channel strip controls, and indeed they share some similar parameters. If you examine the channels a bit more closely, you'll notice that some parameters are shared by all channels, and some groups of channels have different settings.

- **Pitch Bend** - With these controls, offered only on channels 6 and 7, you can control the pitch start point as well as velocity, rate and amount of bend.

- **Tone** -Channels 1, 2 and 10 have this control, which affects the brightness of the drum sound.

- **Sample Start** - This parameter, available on channels 3, 4, 5, 8 and 9, lets you determine where you'd like the sample to start playing.

Mute, Solo and Play Buttons

At the top of each drum channel are three buttons with which you should be familiar with now. The Mute button, which lights up red when clicked on, will completely cut off the playback volume for that channel. The Solo button, yellow when selected, will automatically mute all other channels so you can hear the playback from that channel only. The Play button triggers a single playback of the sample loaded for that channel. This is an excellent way to preview what that individual drum element sounds like.

Effect Sends 1 and 2

The Redrum allows you to use the effects set up in the Remix's Aux Sends 1 and 2 to alter drum sample sounds. Turning the Send knob all the way to the left will offer no effect mix. Turning it to the right will blend more and more effect into your sample. Let's try adding an effect device so we can use these Redrum effect sends.

1. Press Tab to toggle the rack over to view the back.

2. Right click anywhere on the Remix mixer and from the menu that appears choose Create > RV-7 Digital Reverb. This will place the RV-7 device between the mixer and the drum machine.

Take a moment to look at the patching. Notice that the Redrum has its Send Out (both 1 and 2) connected to the Remix's Chaining Aux. This is how Redrum takes advantage of the Remix's effects sends. Notice that the RV-7 we just created has its outputs patched directly to the mixer's number one left and right returns. Remix's Channel 1 (left) Aux Send is patched to the RV-7's input, but the right channel is not. Let's connect that now using a method not used in our earlier chapter.

1. Position your mouse over Remix's number 1 Aux Send Right.

2. Right click on it to bring up the menu and choose Reverb 1 > Right. Instantly a cable is created connecting our Remix's Aux Send 1 Right to the RV-7's Right Input.

3. Press Tab to toggle to the front view.

4. On Redrum's channel 1, press the Play button to trigger drum sample 1. Listen to the sound of the kick bass.

5. Turn the S1 knob to the 3 o'clock position.

6. Press the Trigger button again to listen to the sound of the sample with reverb added.

Pan

Using this knob, you can pan the sample from left to right --
but only if it is a stereo sample. This will be indicated if the
light above the knob (and between S1 and S2) is lit red.

Level

As with every device, the Level knob controls overall
channel volume.

Velocity

The Velocity knob can affect the volume depending on its
alignment. If it's set at the neutral or twelve o'clock position,
the volume will be constant and the Level control will fully
affect volume. If you rotate the knob to the left to create a
negative value, then the higher the velocity, the lower the
volume will be. Rotating the knob to the right will give a
positive value, which means the volume will increase the
higher the velocity is.

Length and the Decay/Gate Switch

Based on how you set this switch, the Length knob will
control how long a sample is heard. When the switch is in its
"up" position, called Gate mode (indicated by a square
wave), the sample will play for as long as you have
determined it will play using the Length knob. The sample
will be cut off abruptly at the end of this period. With the
switch in the "down" position, called Decay mode (with a
gradually down-sloping wave symbol), the sound will fade
out based on the length you have set with the knob.

Pitch

By dialing this knob left, you lower the pitch by up to one
octave. Dialing right raises pitch by up to one octave.

Select

Activate this button when programming the Step buttons.

Bend (found only on channels 6 and 7)

Rotating this knob to the left (for a negative value) means you wish the sample to start with a low pitch that will return to the normal value over time. Turning the knob to the right will start your sample at a higher pitch that will return to normal over time.

Rate (found only on channels 6 and 7)

This knob controls the amount of time it will take for your pitch (changed by the Bend knob) to return to the original value.

Velocity (found only on channels 6 and 7)

Tied to the bend amount, this knob determines the effect of velocity on that parameter. When turned left (for a negative value), the less velocity there is, the more the pitch will bend. When you turn this knob to the right, that value is inverted.

Start (found only on channels 3, 4, 5, 8 and 9)

By turning this knob, you can define where in the sample you wish it to start playing.

Velocity (found only on Channels 3, 4, 5, 8 and 9)

When this knob – tied to the sample start parameter – is turned to the right, the greater the velocity, the later the start will be.

Tone (found only on Channels 1, 2 and 10)

Turing the Tone knob right or left will add or remove audio "brightness."

Velocity (found only on Channels 1, 2 and 10)

This knob links velocity with tone brightness. For a brighter tone turn knob right. For a darker tone turn it left.

The Pattern Settings

This part of the interface, taking up the bottom portion of the Redrum, is where we find the pattern sequencer.

Enable Pattern Section

When you turn this button on, it will glow red and activate Redrum's built-in pattern sequencer. When this button is turned off, this function is disengaged, and you can control the drum machine with the main sequencer or use the attached MIDI keyboard to "play" the different drum sounds.

Mute Button

If you activate the Mute button for the Redrum unit, a red light will appear in the name column and the unit's output will be dampened.

Pattern

Deselecting the Pattern Enable switch (turning the red light off) will eliminate the playback of any patterns you have programmed. When you select the Pattern Enable switch, the pattern will continue playing until it hits the next downbeat.

Pattern and Bank Select

Beneath the Pattern Enable switch are Pattern Select buttons, numbered one to eight, and Bank Select buttons, lettered A through D. These enable you to create a layered drum sound consisting of as many as 32 pattern memories.

Run

The Run button lets you to play back a single pattern based on letter and number combinations selected from the Bank and Pattern Select buttons.

Step Buttons

The Step buttons are a series of 16 buttons at the bottom of Redrum. The "real work" of programming the drum machine comes with activation of the Step buttons at the bottom of Redrum. There are 16 of these. After indicating which sample you'd like to use, you assign it to a Step button and create a pattern of how often you'd like it to be heard.

Steps

You can determine how long a pattern plays before repeating itself by setting a value (the number of steps) from 1 to 64.

Resolution

You control the speed of your pattern playback with this dial.

Shuffle

By activating this button, you apply a "swing" effect to the Redrum. The amount of shuffle is determined by the Pattern Shuffle knob found in the Reason transport.

Edit Steps

Although only 16 Step buttons appear on the interface, in actuality Redrum is capable of 64. You can indicate which group of steps you wish to program by toggling the Edit Steps switch to edit steps 1-16, 17-32, 33-48 or 49-64.

Dynamic

Using this switch, you can make any of your steps play at one of three dynamics -- hard, medium or soft. Use the velocity switch on the individual drum channels to tweak

Multiple Steps

You can select multiple Step buttons by holding your mouse button down and dragging across the region of buttons you wish to select (or deselect). When the Dynamic is set at Medium, you can use keyboard shortcuts -- Shift-clicking to create Hard values on the Step buttons or Alt-clicking to select Soft values.

Flam

Flam is a special drumming effect -- the creation of a quick second strike to a drum element. This draws attention to that step, creating an "accent" and additional rhythm. You select a step for flam by clicking the small red light above the Step button, turning it on. The Flam knob determines the amount of time between the first and second strike. As the knob is rotated from left to right, we go from less to more time between strikes.

Programming a Pattern

To program a pattern, let's use the setup we have created from previous exercises with the Mixer, Redrum and RV-7 devices.

1. Use the Play (trigger) button at the top of each drum channel to preview the sound of each drum element.

2. Make sure that the Enable Pattern and Pattern buttons are activated -- lit red.

3. Click on the 'A' Bank select button. It will glow red.

4. Click on the '1' Pattern select button. It will glow red.

5. For the rest of the pattern parameters leave Steps at 16, Resolution at 1/16, Edit Steps at 1-16 and Dynamic at the Medium level.

6. Click on the Select button of drum channel 1. It will glow yellow.

7. Now click on Step buttons 1, 3, 5, 7, 9, 11, 13 and 15. They will all glow yellow.

8. Press the Run button, and it will light up red. You will hear your first program being played! Press Run again to stop the playback.

9. Press the Select button on drum channel 8. Notice that when you do so, all of the step button lights go out.

10. Select the same step buttons as in instruction 7.

11. Press the Select button on drum channel 9.

12. Now click on Step buttons 2, 4, 6, 8, 10, 12, 14 and 16.

13. Press Run. You can now hear your pattern with three drum elements being played. Let's tweak it a bit so the hi-hats are played softer and the bass harder.

14. With drum channel 9 still selected, move the Dynamic button to soft. Click on all the lit buttons. Notice they change from yellow to green.

15. Press the Select button of drum channel 8, then repeat the previous instructions to change the dynamic of those drum steps.

16. Now press drum channel 1's Select button.

17. Move the Dynamic switch to hard.

18. Press all the lit buttons. They will change to red.

19. Press Run. Notice that now the bass drum is more prominent than the hi-hats sounds. You can build more drum patterns and set them up on different Bank and Pattern buttons (for example A2, A3, A4... A8, B1, B2..., etc.)

Manipulating Patterns

Patterns can be cut, copied, pasted and deleted as easily as text in a word processor. Right click on Redrum to bring up the menu to access these functions.

Adding Some Flam

Let's add some flam using our current pattern setup.

1. Click on drum channel 1's Select button to activate it.

2. Click above Step buttons 1 and 9 to reveal the small red lights.

3. Turn the Flam knob to the 2 o'clock position.

4. Press Run. Notice the accent created by using flam with this pattern.

Copying Your Pattern to the Sequencer Timeline

You may have noticed that unlike the other devices in Reason 3.0, you can't record the drum patterns you've created in the sequencer timeline. Also, while you can save the drum patches (including changes to drum channel parameters), you cannot save the patterns themselves. Instead, what we do is copy the patterns into the timeline.

1. Select the pattern you wish to copy to the timeline using the Bank Select and Pattern Select buttons.

2. Right click anywhere on the Redrum. Select Copy Pattern to Track.

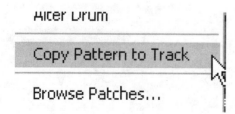

The drum pattern will be copied between the left and right locators in the timeline.

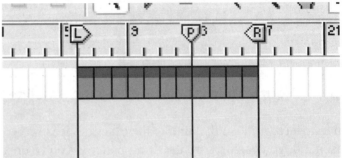

3. Click on the Arrange/Edit button to toggle to Edit mode.

4. Select the Drum and Velocity lane. You can now view the drum patterns as notes in the timeline and can group and edit them as you wish.

One at a Time

You can only copy one pattern at a time to the timeline. If you wish to copy another, just select the appropriate Bank Select and Pattern Select buttons and repeat the previous instructions.

Additional Pattern Functions

Redrum has additional functions that allow you to play with the pattern you have or create new ones. You can access these functions by right clicking on the Redrum interface or using the Edit menu.

- **Shift Pattern Left/Right** - This moves all the drum notes in your pattern one step right or left.

- **Shift Drum Left/Right** - This moves only the drum notes for the selected drum channel either one step left or right.

- **Randomize Pattern** - This builds a totally random pattern based on the patch you have loaded.

- **Randomize Drum** - The creates a random pattern for the selected drum channel only.

- **Alter Pattern** - This changes an existing pattern by randomly moving the drum sounds around.

- **Alter Drum** - This changes a selected drum track by moving its pattern setup.

Shift Pattern Left
Shift Pattern Right
Shift Drum Left
Shift Drum Right

Randomize Pattern
Randomize Drum

Alter Pattern
Alter Drum

The Matrix Pattern Sequencer

There are quite a few similarities between the Matrix and the Redrum, particularly in the functionality of the pattern sequencer. The main difference between them is that the Matrix is a pattern sequencer only and does not generate sounds of its own. In this sense it is a particularly unique device in the Reason 3.0 pantheon. It allows us to take any sound-generating module within Reason and sequence the sound created by that device in the same way we just created drum tracks with Redrum. Let's start by setting everything up, beginning with an empty rack.

1. Right click in the empty rack and create a Mixer 14:2.

2. Right click on the Remix mixer and create a SubTractor Analog Synthesizer.

3. Right click on the SubTractor and create a Matrix Pattern Sequencer.

4. Press Tab to flip the rack over.

Given the order in which we created the devices, the SubTractor is routed to Remix's channel 1 while the mixer is sent to the audio hardware output. Notice the connections between the SubTractor and Matrix. From the Subtractor's Sequencer Control inputs we have connections leading from Gate and CV to the Matrix's Gate CV and Note CV. This means the Matrix is controlling the SubTractor. Up until now, when we were discussing routing, it was specifically about moving the audio signal around. In the case of the Matrix, we're dealing with patterns, so the information we're routing isn't an audio signal but rather "triggering" or CV data. CV stands for "control voltage," a term that originated in the time of the early analog synthesizers before MIDI and digital equipment. In Reason, CV data contains information about what notes to play, when to play them, their velocity and so on. Sometimes a part of the CV signal is separated into Gate data. Typically, the Gate information controls the length of time notes are played as well as the level (or velocity) while the CV indicates which notes should be played.

Matrix Pattern Sequencer Interface

Having recently covered the Redrum, you'll find quite a few function similarities between the two devices. They include…

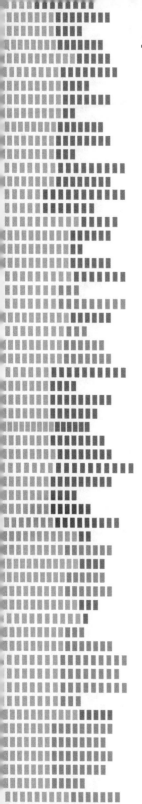

- Pattern Enable switch

- Mute button

- Pattern and Bank select buttons

- Run button

- Resolution knob

- Step controls

- Shuffle

These all work identically to the Redrum. Some additional functions are:

- **Curve/Keys Switch** - This gives you the choice of how to enter your pattern in the Pattern window.

- **Tie** - By activating this button (it will turn red), you can create longer notes within your pattern. You can also create tied notes by holding down the shift key while adjusting gate values. When you use tied notes, the velocity bars (at the bottom of the Pattern window) appear twice as thick.

- **Octave** - Use this button to select the region to which you'd like to program notes, within a five octave range.

Programming a Pattern with the Matrix

For our first example we will use the SubTractor to generate a sound we will program with the Matrix. We will use the routing setup we created earlier.

1. On the SubTractor click on the Browse Patch button to load a patch.

2. From the Reason Factory Sound Bank browse to SubTractor Patches > Bass > and load BassQue.zyp by double clicking on it or selecting it and pressing the OK button.

3. On the Matrix activate the Pattern button so it glows red (if it is not already activated) and select Bank A and Pattern Select 1.

4. Make sure the Curve/Keys switch is set to Keys.

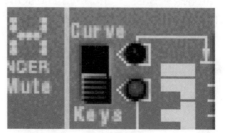

5. Set the Octave switch to 2, the Resolution knob to 1/8 and Steps to 20.

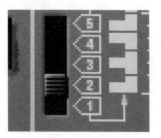

6. Using your pointer, set up the pattern shown here.

We've kept the same note playing to illustrate the effect of changing gate value. You'll notice that as we decrease the gate value, the volume becomes lower, fading out. Then it "fades up." Experiment by programming different note and velocity values across the various octave ranges, as well as adjusting the parameters for resolution, steps, shuffle and tie.

Programming a Pattern with the Matrix Using Curve Values

Note data is not the only thing that can be programmed in the Matrix. Using curved patterns can also create programs that work with non-note data to generate modulation. In these instances the curve CV signals can act as gate triggers indicating when a certain sound or parameter (such as envelope) should be engaged. To create a pattern using curve value, we need to do a bit of rerouting between the SubTractor and Matrix.

1. Press Tab to view the rear of the rack.

2. Right click on the Matrix Curve CV output and from the menu select SubTtractor > Oscillator Pitch Modulation Input. This means the Matrix will control the oscillator pitch modulation.

3. Press Tab to view the front of the rack.

4. Right click in the Pattern window and select Clear Pattern to remove what you'd created earlier.

> Copy Pattern
>
> Paste Pattern
>
> Clear Pattern
>
> Shift Pattern Left

5. Switch the Curve/Keys button to Curve.

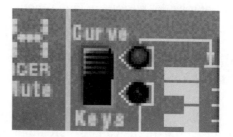

6. On the SubTractor make the Osc 1 and Filter 1 setting match the illustration here.

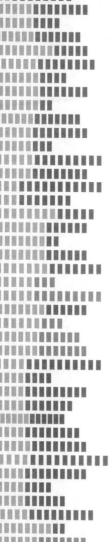

7. Set the Matrix up as seen in this illustration.

8. Click Run.

Notice how the curve setup in the Pattern window determines the triggering of the Osc 1 sound. Note also that the Octave switch does not affect anything in this mode. As you are experimenting with creating a pattern with curves, try patching the curve CV to some of the other modulation inputs on the SubTractor.

Other Matrix Functions

The process for copying your pattern to the sequencer timeline is identical to the method used with the Redrum. You'll find other function similarities in the Edit menu or by right clicking on the Matrix to bring up the menu. These are:

- Cut, Copy, Clear and Paste Pattern

- Shift Pattern Left/Right

- Randomize Pattern

- Alter Pattern

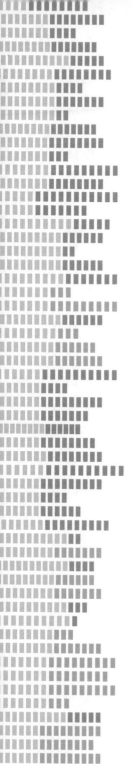

The Shift Pattern Up/Down option will raise or lower your entered note values by one semi-tone when you are in Keys mode.

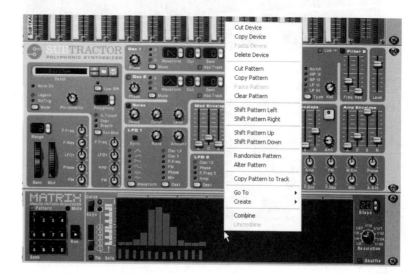

Effects Devices 7

Having covered all the major sound generating and pattern devices in Reason 3.0, it's time we focused our attention on effects devices. Within the sound modules themselves, there are many options for altering, modifying and essentially changing the way our signal sounds. The effects processors take us to the next level, allowing us to thoroughly alter our sound by adding:

- **Filters**

- **Modulation Effects (Flanger, Chorus, Phaser)**

- **Distortion**

- **Dynamic Effects (Compression)**

- **Reverb**

- **And Many Others...**

To demonstrate how these work, we will create a base setup using the Remix mixer and the SubTractor, then add the effect device. Start each effect example with this setup unless suggested otherwise.

1. Starting with an empty rack, right click in the empty area to open the menu and select Mixer 14:2.

Combinator

Mixer 14:2

Line Mixer 6:2

SubTractor Analog Synthesizer

2. Right click on the empty area of the rack and select SubTractor Analog Synthesizer.

Mixer 14:2

Line Mixer 6:2

SubTractor Analog Synthesizer

Malstrom Graintable Synthesizer

NN19 Digital Sampler

3. Right click on the empty area of the rack and add your desired effects device.

Following this method will create a properly patched insert edit.

Dry/Wet

Throughout this effects chapter you will come across devices that have a knob called Dry/Wet. This controls the balance between the unprocessed signal and the signal with the effect applied. The dry condition (with this knob turned to the left) means there is no effect, just audio signal, while wet (knob turned to the right) means the audio signal is given the full desired effect. Anywhere in between will be a balance of dry and wet. Whenever you connect these effects devices, it is important to turn the knob all the way to the wet position. This is so you can control the balance of the effected signal in the mixer using the AUX send knobs. In addition, every effects device has a switch on its left side that enables you to turn the device on or off, or bypass it -- which will allow the audio signal to pass through the device with no effect being applied so you can hear the pre-processed sound.

The RV-7 Digital Reverb

The RV-7 Digital Reverb Processor allows you to choose from 11 reverb algorithms that create the effect of being in certain acoustical settings, from a small enclosed space to a large hall plus many more. Specifically, you can choose:

- Hall

- Large Hall

- Hall 2

- Large Room

- Medium Room

- Small Room

- Gated

- Low Density

- Stereo Echoes

- Pan Room

Use the up and down arrows next to the display showing the currently selected algorithm to choose the one you desire. There are four parameters you can adjust to control different aspects of the algorithms.

Size

This dial controls the virtual room size of the algorithm. The default setting is at the 12 o'clock (or zero) position. Turn the knob to the left (for a negative value) to make the room "smaller" or the right for the opposite effect.

Decay

This dial controls the duration of the reverb. As with the Size knob, zero is the default position. Turn the knob to the right for a greater amount of decay (longer reverb fade-out time) or to the left for the opposite effect.

Damp

The Damp dial will cut higher frequencies out of your reverb. If the knob is dialed all the way to the left, there will be no high frequency cutoff, and as you rotate more to the right, more higher frequencies will be eliminated.

Creating an Ethereal, Reverb Sound.

1. Make sure the SubTractor is selected by clicking on it.

2. Right click the empty area of the rack and from the menu choose RV-7 Digital Reverb. This will add the RV-7 unit and auto-patch it for you.

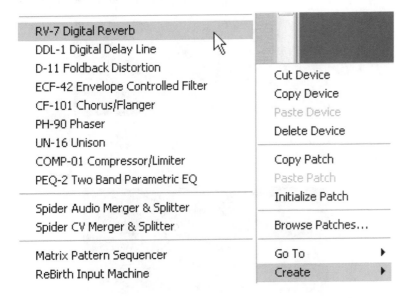

306

3. On the SubTractor, click the Browse Patch icon and browse to Reason Factory Sound Bank > SubTractor Patches > PolySynths > Christmas.zyp. Double click on this or click OK to load this patch.

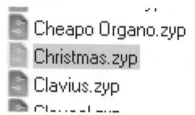

4. On the RV-7 use the up/down arrows to select Large Hall.

5. Turn the Size and Decay knobs to the 1 o'clock position.

6. Keep the damp at 12 o'clock and turn the Dry/Wet knob all the way to the right.

7. Press a few keys on your keyboard to hear the ethereal sound.

8. Dial back the Dry/Wet knob to dry, then press a few keys to hear the unaffected Christmas patch synth sound. Keep experimenting!

DDL-1 Digital Delay Line

Just as it sounds, the Digital Delay Line works by repeatedly replaying the selected note a certain interval of time later.

- **Delay Time** - Use the up and down arrows to show the amount of time you wish to delay. The value shown here is defined by the unit mode you chose.

- **Unit** - Here you can define the delay mode you wish to use. Choosing Steps will create the effect using a tempo-based time delay (based on the tempo set in the Reason transport) while MS will base the delay on actual time, not tempo.

- **Step Length** - Here we define the length of the actual steps that will be the reference for setting the delay in Steps mode. Choose from 1/16 or 1/8T.

- **Feedback** - Use this knob to define how many times you'd like the note to repeat. When it is turned all the way to the left, there are no repetitions, while all the way to the right produces the maximum number of repeats.

- **Pan** - Twist the knob to the left to pan the delay in that direction, or to the right to pan right.

D-11 Foldback Distortion

For basic, easy-to-assemble distortion, the D-11 is your perfect tool.

- **Amount** - Turn this knob all the way to the left for no distortion, full right for full distortion.

- **Foldback** - Based on the concept of "folding back" the wave-form to create a distortion effect, turning this knob defines the complexity of the wave. The base position is 12 o'clock for a standard flat-type distortion. Turn the knob to the left for lighter distortion and to the right for harsher.

ECF-42 Envelope Controlled Filter

An envelope controlled filter works in two ways. In response to an envelope being triggered, a filter's attributes are applied to the sound. Another way to describe this is to say that when a sound's volume hits a certain level, the filter is engaged, changing the shape of the sound's tone. ECF's are also called auto-wahs as they can create a wah-wah effect but are not controlled through a pedal. In addition, in an ECF there are far more filter options for shaping tone than there are in a regular wah-wah device. The ECF-42 is a bit different from the other effect functions in Reason in that two devices are necessary to utilize all of its capabilities. You need one device (such as the SubTractor or Malström) to generate sound (which will be filtered) and another device (such as the Matrix) to act as the envelope control.

No Devices?

If there is no device connected to the CV inputs for use by the envelope controls, the ECF-42 will act only as a filter.

ECF-42 Filter Parameters

The filter parameters on the ECF-42 are controlled by the first four knobs (and one button) starting at the left of the interface. They offer the same functions as the synthesizer filters.

- Frequency

- Resonance

- Envelope Amount

- Velocity

- Mode

ECF-42 Envelope Parameters

As with all of the parameters in Reason 3.0 that control envelope generators, here we have four dials that control:

- Attack

- Decay

- Sustain

- Release

Above the envelope parameters and next to the word Gate is a small light that will come on when input is received via the Envelope Gate input.

CF-101 Chorus/Flanger

The CF-101 combines two effects. A chorus is created by delaying the audio signal multiple times to create the impression of several instruments playing at once. The "flanger" part of the CF-101 creates a swishing or tunnel-like sound by doubling the wave-forms of a single signal, then slightly offsetting them. (This process is called "phase differencing.") The blend of these effects gives your sound a rich, three dimensional aspect.

- **Decay** - Use this knob to control the amount of decay. Turn left for less decay and right for more.

- **Feedback** - The default for this knob is zero (12 o'clock). At this setting you will hear a straight chorus effect. Dial the knob to the left or right for different distinctly flanger tones.

- **LFO Rate** - Turning this knob from left to right will affect the frequency that is modulating the delay, speeding up the oscillation.

- **LFO Modulation Amount** - Turning this knob from left to right increases the amount of the modulation affecting the delay time.

- **LFO Sync** - Activating this button will make it glow red, which indicates that the LFO frequency is synced to the song tempo set in the Reason transport.

- **Send Mode** - If you have set up the CF-101 as a send effect, activate this button (it will glow red). If it is set up as an insert, make sure it is not activated.

PH-90 Phaser

A phaser creates an effect similar to a flanger but not quite as intense or prominent. A phaser creates its effect by shifting the phase of the frequency mixed with the original signal. The shifting is accomplished with a notch filter (tuned to a very narrow band of frequencies called "notches"), and this sweeps up and down through some of the frequency range. The PH-90 Phaser has six knobs for adjusting the effect.

Frequency

This knob is used to control the first frequency range of the notch filter. Turning it will move the other frequency ranges (notches) as well.

Split

The Split knob defines how much space there is between different notches. Turn it left for less distance between the notches, right for more.

Width

You can determine the frequency range covered by notches using this knob. Turn it to the left for a narrower range, to the right for wider.

LFO Rate

This knob controls the speed of the Low Frequency Oscillator, which is modulating the frequency value set by the Frequency knob. Turn the knob to the left for a slower phaser sweep or to the right for a quicker sweep.

LFO Frequency Modulation

The parameter controlled here is similar to that of a Modulation Amount knob. Turn to the left for less modulation, to the right for more.

LFO Sync

When this button is activated, a red light above it will illuminate, indicating that the LFO values will be synchronized to the song tempo set in the Reason transport.

Feedback

Adjust this parameter to affect the tonality of the effect -- left for less, right for more.

UN-16 Unison

Similar to the chorus effect but with added polyphony, the UN-16 Unison allows you to create the impression of multiple "voices" playing the notes of your instrument.

Voice Count

Use this button to set how many voices you'd like to hear (4.8 or 16).

Detune

Multiple voices are created with the UN-16 by taking the original signal and adding small amounts of delay, tone modulation and low frequency noise. By turning this dial you are determining how "far apart" or detuned these voices are. At the far left the voices will be "closest." At the far right they will be furthest apart.

Comp-01 Auto Make-Up Gain Compressor

A compressor is an amplifier that reduces the dynamic range (the ratio between loudest and quietest parts) of the audio signal. The Comp-01 goes one step beyond in that it adds an automatic gain boost to "make up" the volume reduction of the loudest sounds that have been compressed to fit in the dynamic range.

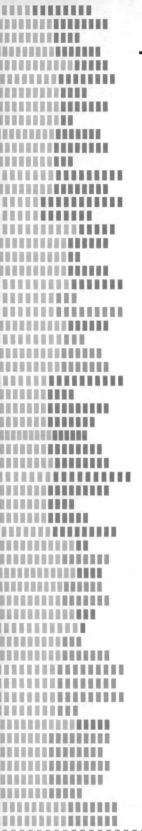

Ratio

With this dial you can set the ratio that determines the dynamic range. When the dial is turned all the way left, the ratio is 1:1, meaning no reduction. By dialing from left to right you can reach a maximum ratio of 16:1. This means that over a pre-determined volume level (set using the Threshold knob) the signal will be reduced by 16 times.

Threshold

This knob defines the crossover point at which we wish the compression to take effect. Volumes above this point will be affected (and compressed) while volumes lower will not be changed. The more the knob is turned to the right, the lower the threshold point, meaning more volume levels will be compressed.

Attack

This parameter is the speed at which compression takes effect once volumes have crossed the threshold level. If the knob is turned to the left, the compression effect will be immediate. The more it is turned to the right, the more time it will take for compression to kick in.

Release

This knob controls the speed at which the Comp-01 disengages the compression after it dips below the threshold. If the dial is set all the way to the left, the effect will be instantaneous. Turning the knob to the right will lengthen the disengagement of compression for a subtler effect.

Gain

Located at the left of the interface is a meter calibrated in dB. This visually indicates the amount of compression (and make-up gain) being applied.

PEQ-2 Two Band Parametric EQ

If you'd like to apply more fine tuned equalization than is available from the Remix, Reason 3.0 includes a two-band equalizer in the PEQ-2. This effect module includes two independent equalizers controlled by three knobs each and a graphic display that shows the frequency response curve created by the knobs. The PEQ-2 is defaulted to work with only one equalizer (controlled by the top set of knobs and labeled A), but you can activate the second equalizer, B, by clicking on the button next to it so its light comes on.

- **Frequency** - The first and left-most knob defines the center frequency you wish to focus on. A left turn of this knob will move the center to the left of the graphic display, which means a lower frequency, while a right turn does the opposite.

- **Q** - This value defines the spread of frequencies to be EQ'd. As you turn the knob from left to right, you will go from isolating a wider range to a narrower range.

- **Gain** - This last knob sets the level by which you wish to boost or reduce isolated frequencies. To increase gain, turn the knob to the right. The curve on the graphic display will push upward to a peak. To reduce gain, turn the knob to the left, and the curve will grow downward as a trough.

The RV-7000 Advance Reverb Processor

The RV-7000 takes us a few steps beyond the capabilities of the RV-7. Beyond just creating the sound of a "location," it also has a number of parameters (and patches) for creating special effects. As an advanced processor, it lets you manipulate many characteristics to customize and enhance reverb, including numerous controls for EQ and Gate functions. It has nine built-in algorithms, each of which can be further tweaked.

RV-7000 Main Panel

The main panel of the RV-7000 allows you to make general or "coarse" changes in reverb parameters.

- **EQ Enable** - Activating this button will turn on the red light next to it and allow you to apply the EQ changes you make in the remote programmer to the wet reverb sound.

- **Gate Enable** - As with the previous button, the red light on this one will go on when the function is activated. In the remote programmer you can configure parameters to trigger the gate to open or close to apply reverb effects in many different scenarios.

- **Decay** - Turning this dial from left to right will increase the duration of the reverb or feedback.

- **HF Damp** - As you rotate the knob from left to right, higher frequencies will fade out faster.

- **HI EQ** - This produces a "shelving-type" equalization. The more the knob is turned to the right, the more high frequencies can be heard for a harder reverb sound.

RV-7000 Remote Programmer

Clicking on the small arrow beneath the Patch window will bring the programmer up. The interface is comprised of a large graphic display surrounded by eight dials. In the lower left corner is the Edit mode button, which gives you three choices: Reverb, EQ or Gate. Depending on which mode you select, not each dial may have a parameter to affect.

Reverb Mode

In Reverb mode you can select any of nine algorithms that will emulate a particular environment, including some special-effect environments.

- Small Space

- Room

- Hall

- Arena

- Plate

- Spring

- Echo

- Multi Tap

- Reverse

Each algorithm you choose will offer unique variables that you can adjust with the eight knobs surrounding the graphic display. Some algorithms may not have eight different parameters to change, so those dials will not be needed.

Algorithm Information

For a highly detailed description of the breakdown of each algorithm (and its individual controls) as well as the specific parameters for each mode (reverb, EQ and gate), please see Reason's documentation.

EQ Mode

Activate EQ mode by clicking on the Edit mode button until a red light glows next to EQ. The image in the graphic display will change to illustrate the band of frequencies affected by the EQ. The purpose of EQ with the RV-7000 is to specifically enhance the reverb using two EQ bands, a full band parametric EQ and a low frequency shelving type EQ. In total five parameters can be adjusted:

- Low Gain

- Low Frequency

- Parametric Gain

- Parametric Frequency

- Parametric Q

Gate Mode

Click on the Edit button until a red light glows next to Gate. The image in the graphic display will change to illustrate two meters: a signal meter showing Level/Threshold and the second showing the Gate status. Seven parameters can be used to customize Gate mode:

- Threshold

- Decay Modulation

- Triggering Source

- High Pass

- Attack

- Hold

- Release

Creating a Reverb Effect Using the RV-7000

1. On the Sub Tractor, click on the Load Patch icon and browse to the Reason Factory Sound Bank > SubTractor Patches > Polysynths > GlassOrgan.zyp. This will give us a cathedral-like organ sound.

2. Click on the arrow on the RV-7000 to open the remote programmer.

3. Press the Edit button so that Reverb is selected (if it is not already so).

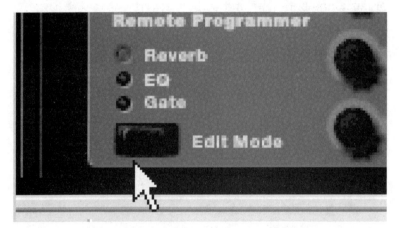

4. Turn the first knob on the programmer (Controlling Algorithm) to select Arena.

5. Press a few keys on your keyboard to hear the sound of the organ as if it were being played in an arena.

6. On the main panel, flip the On/Off/Bypass switch to bypass, then play a few keys on your keyboard to hear the organ sound both with and without reverb.

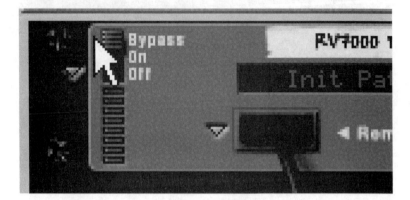

7. Turn the On/Off/Bypass switch back to on.

8. On the remote programmer turn the Right Delay knob (top right) to the right so it reads 850ms. This will increase the delay, making the arena sound larger and more "echoey."

9. Press the Edit button to select EQ.

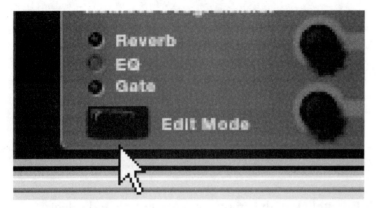

10. Using the knobs to the right of the graphic display, adjust the Param Gain to 16.3 dB, the Param Freq to 3623 Hz and the Param Q to 0.2. This will create a gentle EQ boost in the higher frequency range and will tweak your reverb sound.

The BV512 Vocoder

A "vocoder" is one of the most unique devices in Reason 3.0. It helps you make instruments "sing." How? It starts with two audio input sources, one called a carrier and the other the modulator. The carrier represents the instrument sound that will be altered by the frequency characteristics of the modulator signal. This process gives a singing quality to instrument sounds. The setup for this can be quite elaborate, so let's start by departing from our basic effects setup and building a vocoded sound effect from an empty rack.

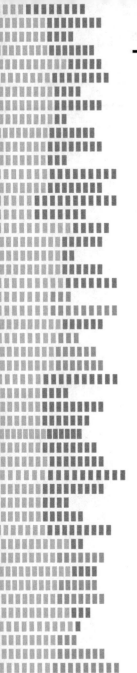

Initial Vocoder Device Setup

1. Right click in the empty area to open the menu and select Mixer 14:2.

Combinator

Mixer 14:2
Line Mixer 6:2

SubTractor Analog Synthesizer

2. Right click in the empty area of the rack and select SubTractor Analog Synthesizer from the menu.

Mixer 14:2
Line Mixer 6:2

SubTractor Analog Synthesizer
Malstrom Graintable Synthesizer
NN19 Digital Sampler

3. Right click in the empty area to open the menu and select BV512 Vocoder.

RV7000 Advanced Reverb
Scream 4 Distortion
BV512 Digital Vocoder

RV-7 Digital Reverb
DDL-1 Digital Delay Line

4. Right click in the empty area and create a NN-19 Sampler.

SubTractor Analog Synthesizer
Malstrom Graintable Synthesizer
NN19 Digital Sampler
NN-XT Advanced Sampler
Dr.REX Loop Player
Redrum Drum Computer

5. Right click in the empty area and create Matrix Pattern Sequencer.

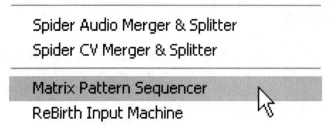

Spider Audio Merger & Splitter

Spider CV Merger & Splitter

Matrix Pattern Sequencer

ReBirth Input Machine

Vocoder Routing Setup

Essentially most of our routing is done, but we need change a few things to make this work.

1. Press Tab to flip the rack over to rear view.

2. Right click on the NN-19 Left Audio Output and from the menu select Vocoder > Modulator Input.

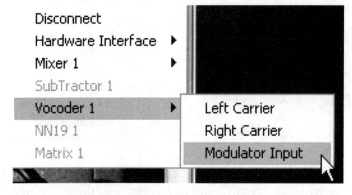

Disconnect
Hardware Interface ▶
Mixer 1 ▶
SubTractor 1
Vocoder 1 ▶   Left Carrier
NN19 1   Right Carrier
Matrix 1   Modulator Input

3. Right click on the NN-19 Right Audio Output and from the menu select Disconnect.

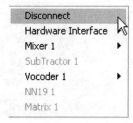

Disconnect
Hardware Interface
Mixer 1 ▶
SubTractor 1
Vocoder 1 ▶
NN19 1
Matrix 1

4. Press Tab again to flip the rack to front view.

Creating a Repeating Vocal Sound for Our Modulator

To make the carrier sing properly in this example, we need to create a repeating voice-like song sound to act as a modulator. We will do this using the NN-19 to generate the voice sound and the Matrix to repeat the sound.

1. Click on the Browse Patch icon on the NN-19 and browse to Reason Factory Sound Bank > NN-19 Patches > Voice > OHHCHOIR.smp. Double click on it or select OK to load this sample.

2. Press Run on the Matrix. We're just using the Matrix as a device to create repetition of our sample, so there's no need to modify it. At this point, though, we still won't hear anything.

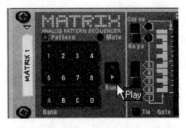

3. Notice on the BV512 Vocoder that both modulation meters (one on the left and the orange one in the center of the interface) are showing levels. Turn the Dry/Wet knob fully to the left and, as you do, you will hear the Ohhchoir sample playing continuously.

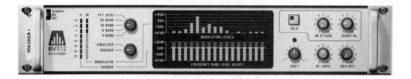

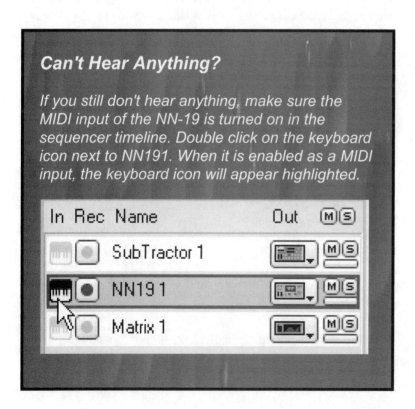

Can't Hear Anything?

If you still don't hear anything, make sure the MIDI input of the NN-19 is turned on in the sequencer timeline. Double click on the keyboard icon next to NN191. When it is enabled as a MIDI input, the keyboard icon will appear highlighted.

Creating a Carrier Sound You Wish to Make Sing

1. Turn the BV512 vocoder dry/wet knob fully to the right.

2. On the SubTractor click on the Browse Patch icon and browse to Reason Factory Sound Bank > SubTractor Patches > PolySynths > String Machine.zyp.

3. In the sequencer timeline click on the keyboard icon in the IN column next to SubTractor 1 to activate it as the MIDI input.

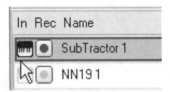

4. On the Matrix pattern sequencer press Run (if it was stopped previously).

5. Press a few keys on your keyboard to hear the string machine sound modulated by the OhhChoir to make it sing! To hear the difference between the vocoded sound and the un-effected SubTractor patch, toggle the Bypass/On/Off button between on and bypass.

If you find the effect too subtle, try using the Select Next/Previous Patch arrow buttons in the NN-19 to go through the list of loaded samples, which will modulate the string machine in a different way. Then try loading different samples on the SubTractor (carrier) side to hear how they can be modulated so as to "sing."

The BV512 Vocoder Interface

After the rather complicated setup, you'll likely find the interface of the BV512 straightforward. Here is a look at the interface from left to right.

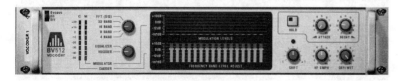

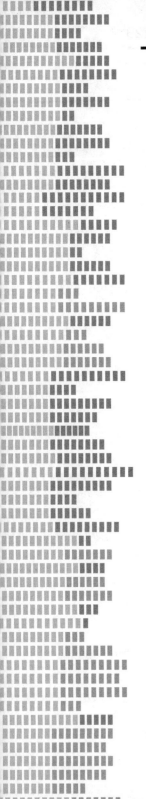

Carrier/Modulation Level Meters

These two meters will show the volume level of Carrier (on the left) and Modulator (on the right).

Equalizer/Vocoder Switch

The BV512 is a dual function device in that it can act as both a vocoder and an equalizer. When you switch this knob to Equalizer, you are affecting EQ on the Carrier signal only.

Band Switch

This knob controls the amount of filter bands you wish to view in the Modulation Levels and Frequency Band Level Adjust displays.

Modulation Levels and Frequency Band Level Adjust Displays

The large display with orange graphics in the center of the interface is divided into two sections, upper and lower. The upper section, called Modulation Levels, shows the volume of the signal from the modulation source across a spectrum of frequencies. The lower section, called Frequency Band Level Adjust, consists of a number of bars. The amount depends on the value you select from the Band switch. You can manipulate these bars using your mouse to elevate or lower frequencies.

Reset Band Levels

Right click on the display and select Reset Band Levels from the menu.

Hold button

Activating this button (it's embedded light will glow red) locks the current settings.

Attack knob

Use this knob, active in Vocoder mode, to control the amount of attack. Turn the knob from left to right to go from fast to slow attack.

Decay

Use this knob to control the speed of level fade-out. Turn to the left for faster, to the right for slower.

Shift

Turning this knob will raise or lower the frequency of the carrier's filter levels.

Hi Frequency Emphasis

This knob is used to raise the high frequencies of the carrier's signal.

The Scream 4 Sound Destruction Unit

If you have ever played air guitar, with your eyes pressed closed and imagining yourself shredding the six string on stage in front of thousands of screaming fans, this effect is for you. It is the ultimate distortion box! But truthfully, it's much more than that. It's a sound destruction unit that produces over the top effects, yes, but it also offers subtle warping and distortion effects. We're going to use our standard effects setup, so you should have the Remix and SubTractor already added to the rack. Make sure to click on the SubTractor to select it before adding the Scream 4, so it will be automatically patched. Right click on the SubTractor or empty rack and choose Create > Scream 4 Distortion. It will be automatically patched.

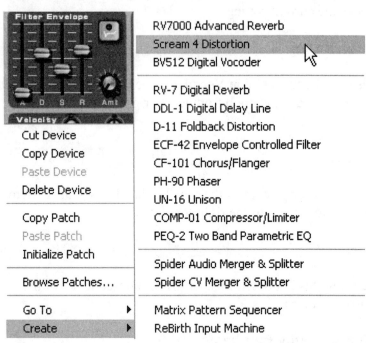

The Scream 4 Sound Destruction Unit Interface

The interface for the Scream 4 can be broken up into three sections: Damage, Cut and Body. In addition, you'll find the usual device controls: Bypass/On/Off switch, Load/Save/Previous/Next patch, and a Master Level control.

Scream Damage Section

Make the controls for this section active by clicking on the light next to the word Damage so it glows yellow. The type and amount of distortion, warping, or general all around destruction of your audio signal is controlled in this section.

- **Damage Control Knob** - This could also be labeled (much less creatively) the "amount knob," for it lets you control how much damage you wish to apply. The more this knob is turned to the right, the greater the destruction.

- **Damage Type Knob** - Scream 4 has ten algorithms that offer a wide range of damage types, including:

  - Overdrive

  - Distortion

  - Fuzz

  - Tube

  - Tape

  - Feedback

  - Modulate

  - Warp

  - Digital

  - Scream

Variables

Each of these has a different set of variables that make the resulting sound quite unique. For a detailed breakdown of each algorithm and a description of the effect and parameters, you can refer to Reason 3.0's documentation.

The P1 and P2 knobs control different parameters based on which algorithm (damage type) you choose. For example, with the Overdrive and Distortion algorithms P1 controls tone, but with Feedback it controls size.

Scream Cut Section

Scream 4 has a very basic three-band equalizer to fine tune your damage. The three sliders, labeled Lo, Mid and Hi, allow you to cut or boost the frequencies of these respective ranges. Remember that boosting the frequencies will raise the overall level while cutting them will lower it.

Scream Body Section

Like the other sections, this one has to be activated by clicking on the light so it turns yellow. The body section contains parameters that give the sound the characteristics of being within a certain type of resonating environment or body.

- **Body Type Knob** - This knob has five settings that enable you to select a body type (acoustic environment).

- **Body Resolution Knob** - Dialing this knob from left to right will increase the resonance.

- **Body Scale Knob** - This knob defines the size of the environment. Turning the knob to the left increases the size while turning it to the right decreases the size.

- **Auto Knob** - This controls a function called "envelope follower effect." Working in conjunction with the Body Scale Knob, you can use this control to increase the scale setting the louder the incoming signal is. The effect is similar to a wah-wah pedal. Turn this knob clockwise to increase the amount of follower envelope effect.

Creating a Fuzzy Bass Guitar Effect

1. Click on the Browse Patch icon on the SubTractor and browse to the Reason Factory Sound Bank > Sub Tractor Patches > Bass > BassGuitar.zyp. This will load the bass guitar sound.

2. Turn on all sections of the Scream 4, Damage, Cut and Body.

3. Set your damage control to 3 o'clock.

4. Set the Damage Type knob to Fuzz and the P1 and P2 knobs to the 3 o'clock position.

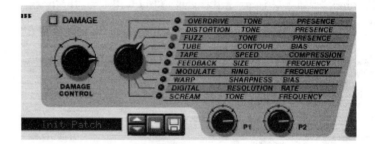

5. Raise the Lo slider in the Cut section so it is at the first hash mark above the midpoint.

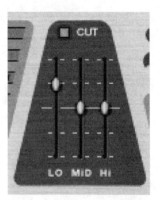

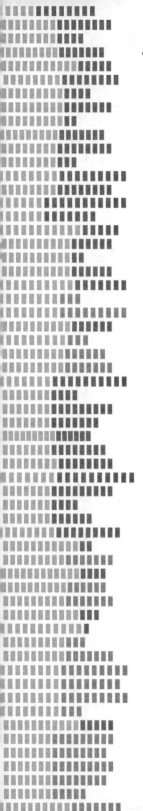

6. In the Body section turn the Reso and Scale knobs to 2 o'clock, the Auto knob to 3 o'clock and the Body Type knob to D.

Spider Audio Merger and Splitter

Add a Spider Audio Merger and Splitter to your rack setup. (Create menu > Spider Audio Merger & Splitter). At first glance, you'll notice that this function is unlike any others in Reason 3.0. The spider does not generate or add effects to an audio signal. There are no knobs or buttons on the front of the device, just lights to indicate when the signal is being passed through inputs.

COMP-01 Compressor/Limiter

PEQ-2 Two Band Parametric EQ

Spider Audio Merger & Splitter
Spider CV Merger & Splitter

Matrix Pattern Sequencer

Press the Tab key to flip the rack over. As its name indicates, the spider has two features:

- **Audio Merging** - This consolidates four stereo inputs into one stereo output. You can see this on the left side of the back of the spider.

- **Audio Splitting** - This splits a single stereo input into four stereo outputs.

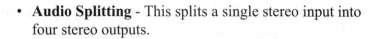

Spider and Mono

The spider can also take mono inputs. On the merger side, any mono connection inserted into any of the L/Mono inputs will come out both the left and right outputs. Any mono connection to the R inputs will only come out the R output. On the splitter side, any signal inputted to the L or R inputs will come out all four respective outputs.

Adding Devices and Removing Connections

Let's try an exercise that will examine both merging and splitting the SubTractor's signal so that we can hear it using two effects simultaneously. Start with our basic effects setup, a remix mixer and the SubTractor.

1. Using either the Create menu or right clicking in the rack, add these three devices: RV-7 Digital Reverb, DDL-1 Digital Delay Line and Spider Audio Merger and Splitter.

2. Press the Tab key to flip the rack.

3. Disconnect all the cables connecting the SubTractor and all of the new devices you've created. Do this by either right clicking on the inputs/outputs and selecting disconnect from the menu or by simply moving the mouse pointer over any of the inputs/outputs and clicking on them, then dragging them out to "unplug" them. When you disconnect a cable at one end, it will automatically disconnect it at the other. The end result should be no cables connecting any of the four devices.

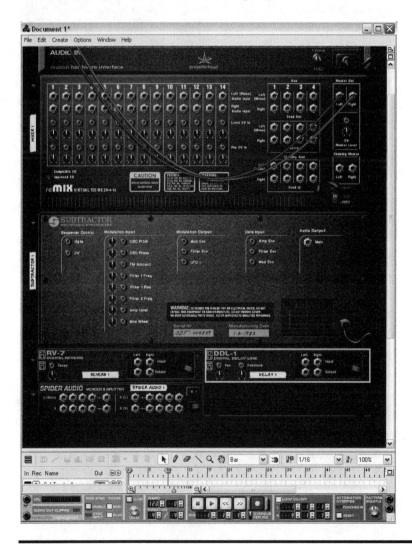

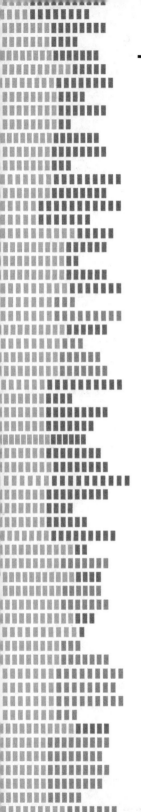

Using the Merger to Create a Stereo Output

The SubTractor is a mono output device, but in using the merger we will take its mono input and spit it out as two (R and L) signals.

1. Right click on the SubTractor Audio Output Main and from the menu select Spider Audio 1 > Merge Input 1 Left.

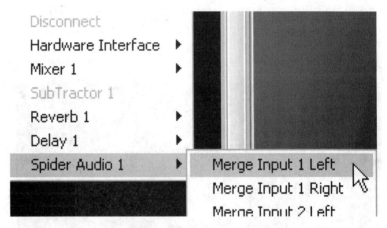

Now we will route the "stereo" output from the merger to the stereo input of the splitter.

2. Move your pointer to the Merge Output Left connector and click and hold your mouse button down. Drag your pointer right to the Split Input Left [A (L)] and release the mouse button. A cable will be created between these two ports.

3. Repeat instruction 2 from Merge Output Right to Split Input Right [A (R)].

Connecting the Split Output to the Effects Devices

1. Right click on the Split Output 1 Left and from the menu choose Reverb 1 > Left. This will automatically connect both Left and Right outputs from the splitter to the digital reverb effects device.

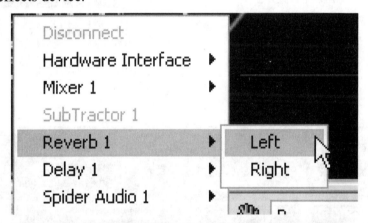

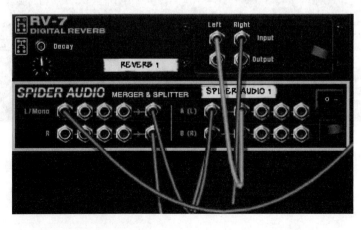

2. Right click on Split Output 2 Left and from the menu choose Delay 1 > Left. This will automatically connect both Left and Right outputs from the splitter to the digital delay line effects device.

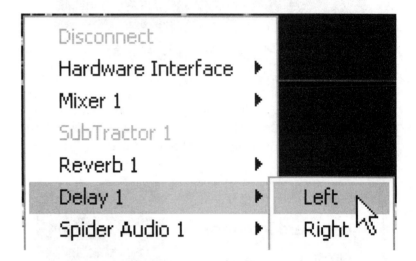

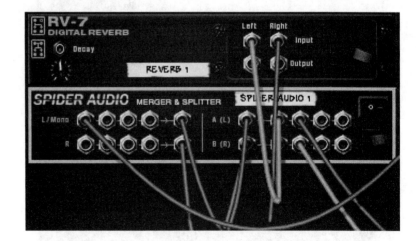

Connecting the Effects Devices to Separate Mixer Channels

1. On the RV-7 right click on the Left Output port and from the menu select Mixer 1 > Channel 1 Left. Both your left and right outputs will be patched to the mixer's channel 1.

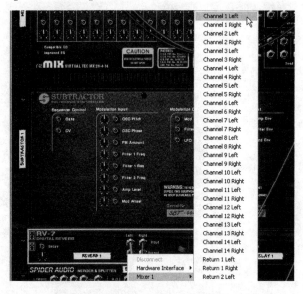

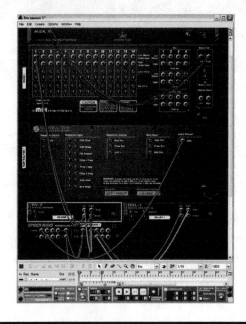

2. On the DDL-1 right click on the Left Output port and from the menu select Mixer 1 > Channel 2 Left. Both your left and right outputs will be patched to the mixer's channel 2.

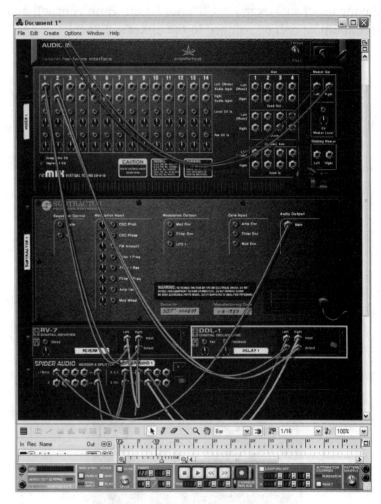

3. Trying playing a few keys on your keyboard. You will hear the SubTractor's output simultaneously being played with both a reverb and a digital delay effect!

Spider CV Merger and Splitter

In effect this spider works exactly like its audio sibling, with the exception that the data being split or merged is not audio signals but rather CV information.

- **CV Merger and CV Splitter** - Up to four individual CV inputs can be merged for one CV output. With the CV Splitter, each splitter (Split A and B) can accept one CV input,which can be split into three distinct outputs, with the fourth output being an inverted value.

The MClass Effects

These five features, brand new to Reason 3.0, are designed to help you master your song in preparation for output and distribution. Mastering is about finessing and getting that final polish that takes your creation it to the perfect place -- readiness for your fans to hear!

MClass Equalizer

With the MClass Equalizer you get five equalizers rolled into one: three shelving and two parametric equalizers. At the top of the interface you'll find the EQ name (which tells you the type of EQ) as well as the frequency range it covers. In addition, at the top of each equalizer is an on/off button that glows red when it is turned on -- so you can select any combination of types you wish. Like its little sibling the PEQ-2, this equalizer has a graphic display that shows the effect of the parameter settings on the frequency response curve.

Control Knobs

The last four equalizers all have Frequency, Gain and Q parameter control knobs that function in the same way as their counterparts on the PEQ-2 do, the only difference being the frequency range covered.

- *Lo Cut - Applying this EQ will remove all frequencies below 30 Hz.*

- *Lo Shelf - This equalizer removes frequencies from 30 to 600Hz using a shelving method.*

- *Param 1 - When this EQ method is activated, frequencies surrounding the center frequency selection range from 39Hz to 20kHz.*

- *Param 2 - This equalizer is identical to Param 1.*

- *Hi Shelf - This equalizer removes frequencies from 3kHz to 12kHz using a shelving method.*

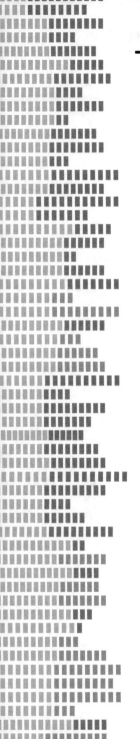

MClass Stereo Imager

A stereo imager is a device that helps enhance the special effect between the left and right stereo channels. The MClass stereo imager allows you to take a specific band of frequencies (low or high) and make their stereo images (the perceived distance between the left and right channels "narrower" or "wider."

- **X-Over Frequency** - Standing for Crossover Frequency, this crucial dial (covering frequencies from 100Hz to 6kHz) allows you to delineate between the frequencies covered by the Lo Band stereo image dial and its Hi Band equivalent. Wherever you set the white line on the dial represents the crossover point. All the frequencies counter-clockwise of this white line (the lower frequencies) will have their stereo image controlled by the Lo Band dial while all frequencies clockwise from it (the higher frequencies) will be affected by the Hi Band dial.

- **Lo Band** - This sets the stereo width of lower frequencies (defined by the X-Over Freq dial). Turn the dial to the left to narrow the stereo image, to the right for the opposite effect. The Lo Band Active light will come on when this dial has been activated.

- **Hi Band** - This works exactly like the High Band dial but covers the higher frequencies as defined by the X-Over Freq dial.

- **Solo Section** - When a button is selected, it will glow red. Choosing Solo Hi Band will allow you to hear only the Hi Band stereo imager. Solo Lo Band does the same for that dial. Choose Normal to hear both the Lo and Hi Band stereo imagers.

> ### It Can't Do It All
>
> *This device is not a miracle worker. It cannot take a mono signal and transform it into stereo!*

MClass Compressor

You'll notice many similarities between controls of the MClass compressor and the Comp-01 we described earlier. As it is designed to be a mastering tool, the MClass offers a very wide range of compression capabilities.

- **Input Gain** - Use this dial together with the Threshold dial to control how much compression you wish to apply to the signal.

- **Threshold** - This one works in the same way as the dial on the Comp-01, with a range of -36 to zero dB.

- **Soft Knee** - Using this feature will apply the compression gradually and gently as the threshold point is approached. Pressing the button will cause it to glow red, meaning the soft knee is activated.

- **Ratio** - This works like the Comp-01 ratio dial but with the added feature of ratios from 1:1 to infinity to 1.

- **Gain** - As with its Comp-01 counterpart, here we can see the amount of reduction applied.

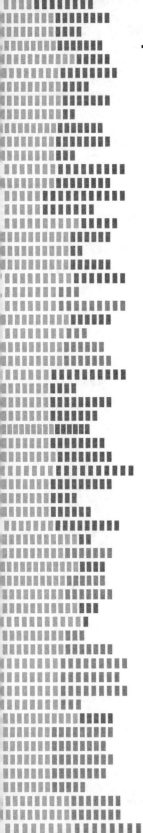

- **Sidechain** - This feature is activated only when a signal is received through the "sidechain inputs" at the back of the MClass compressor. (A red light above the word "Active" on the front of the device will glow.) The signal received by the sidechain is not necessarily meant to be heard. Its primary purpose is to cue the compression to engage. (If you do wish to hear the sidechain input, click on the Solo button.) An example of this might be a part of a song where an instrumental solo ends and vocals begin. Setting up the vocals as the sidechain input will mean that when the singing begins, compression will be applied to the instruments.

- **Attack** - This has the same function as the dial on the Comp-01.

- **Release** - Again, this is the same as Comp-01.

- **Output Gain** - Working as a gain boost, this dial adds volume to the signal whose level was reduced in the compression process.

MClass Maximizer

The MClass maximizer incorporates an audio device called a "limiter." Essentially, this is a compressor with a fixed ratio (usually 10:1 or greater). Its purpose is to allow a boost in loudness without causing distortion. The maximizer also offers a soft clip function, which applies a different kind of limiter creating a soft, warm sound.

- **Input Gain** - Use this knob to control the level of the input signal. Left for less, right for more.

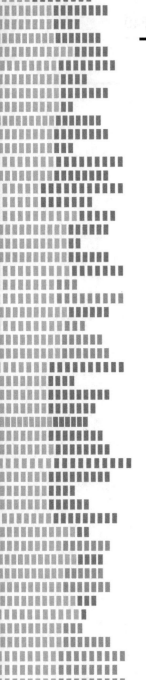

- **Limiter** - This button will glow red when the limiter is turned on.

- **4 ms Look Ahead** - Like the other buttons on the maximizer, this one glows red when activated. Applying a delay of very short duration, the Look Ahead feature allows for moments reaction time to reduce the gain when high level audio spikes are heard.

- **Gain** - This meter will visually indicate the level of the signal with the limiter parameters applied.

- **Attack** - This parameter has three buttons (Fast, Mid and Slow), which indicate the speed at which the limiter takes effect.

- **Release** - The buttons related to this parameter control the speed at which the limiter disengages and the uncompressed signal is heard. Fast, slow and auto buttons will automatically choose the release time based on the varying signal levels.

- **Output Gain** - Use this knob to control the output level of the affected signal.

- **Soft Clip Amount** - When this distortion-adding option is applied, it has a warming effect. Dial the knob from left to right to increase the distortion. With the dial turned all the way to the left, you will have "hard clipping," an instantaneous application of compression. With the dial at the far right, you will have the most distortion and the warmest sound.

- **Output Meter** - This enables you to view audio output levels in one of two forms -- by selecting buttons for either Peak or VU.

MClass Combinator Mastering Suite Combi

The individual MClass effects can be used on their own or in conjunction with one another to help you master your song. A great place to start for those who are new to mastering, or those who are simply looking for "one stop shopping," is the Mastering Suite Combi. This suite (consisting of all four MClass devices) takes advantage of a new Reason 3.0 tool called the Combinator, which we will describe in the next chapter. Whenever you create a new song, along with the Reason hardware interface elements of the rack, a mastering "Combi" will also be created. When this appears in the rack for the first time, it is loaded with the default mastering suite patch, which has a basic setup for controlling the essential parameters necessary for mastering. Reason 3.0 comes with other preset Combi effect patches that you can apply for instant mastering effects appropriate to the genre or type of song you've created. At the more advanced level you can clear the Combi (by right clicking and selecting Init Patch from the menu) and add the specific MClass devices you wish, then program up to four rotary dials and four buttons to control them from the interface. Regardless of what patch setup you apply (custom or preset), there are a few parameters common to all Combi's. Some of these are self-explanatory. Others we will need to describe.

- Browse, Save, Previous/Next patch

- Pitch and Modulation Wheels

- Run Pattern Devices

- Bypass All FX

- **Show Programmer** - Clicking on this button will cause it to glow red and reveal the programmer interface. This will appear just beneath the main Combi interface. Here you can define the rotary dials and buttons on the interface as well as key mapping and modulation routing parameters.

- **Show Devices** - This will reveal the MClass devices nested in the Combinator.

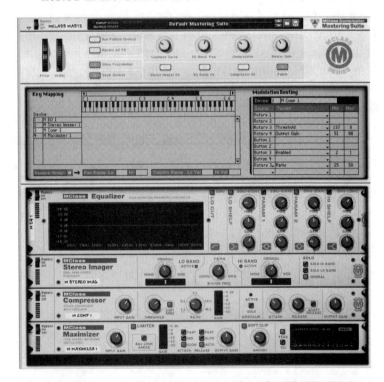

The Combinator and Outputting

8

We'll conclude the Reason 3.0 Complete Course by examining a unique new tool called the Combinator. We'll also learn what we can do once our song is completed, including:

- **Adding Song Information**

- **Publishing the Song**

- **Creating a Self-Contained Song for Collaboration**

- **Exporting the Song as a MIDI or Audio File**

The Combinator

The Combinator allows you to create combinations of multiple devices that will ultimately generate sound (instrument Combi's) or process audio signals with special effects (effect Combi's). As stated in the previous chapter regarding the MClass Mastering Combi, the Combinator interface is highly customizable. There are really no limitations on what you can build with it. Compositions can be elaborate or simple. While the Combinator itself has may components, as it pertains to the rack it is seen as only one device with only one set of audio outputs. This makes it easy to build even extremely elaborate sound or effect setups into your rack.

Combinator or The Rack?

Why use the Combinator instead of just placing the devices in the rack? For one, it makes organizing them much easier, and including the Combinator in the rack is as simple as connecting one device. More importantly, though, it allows you to build a particularly unique sound that you can save as a patch (called a Combi). This makes your signature sound or effects Combi portable to any song you're creating!

How to Create a Combinator

Adding a Combinator to the rack is as simple as creating any other device, and here we will discuss a few methods for building a Combi. We'll start off with a basic setup:

1. Using the Create menu or by right clicking in the empty rack, select Mixer 14:2.

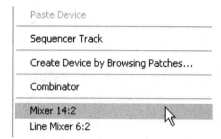

2. Using one of the two methods mentioned in instruction one, select Combinator.

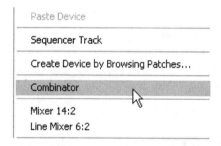

This creates a setup with a Remix mixer and a "blank" Combinator.

The Combinator Interface and Programming

When the Combinator display window shows Init Patch, you are working with an essentially blank Combinator canvas. Let's take a moment to examine the interface. Across the top of the Combinator we find the usual On/Off/Bypass switch, a display window that will show output levels, notes on and external routing indicators as well as the name of the currently loaded Combinator patch. In addition, there are the usual Browse/Save Patch buttons and Select Previous/Next Patch buttons. If we click on the minimize arrow to the left of the On/Off/Bypass switch, we can hide other interface buttons and dials. There are six fixed and eight customizable parameters on the Combinator.

- **Pitch and Modulation Wheels** - Find these at the left of the Combinator and use them to control the overall effect of pitch and output modulation on your combined devices.

- **Run Pattern Devices** - When you turn on this button, all pattern devices in the Combinator will have their Run buttons activated.

- **Bypass All FX** - This will switch every effect device within the Combinator to bypass mode.

- **Show Programmer** - Activate this button to reveal the programming window.

- **Show Devices** - When you turn this button on, all the Combinator's devices will be visible, bounded by a white box. Turning this button off will hide the devices.

There are four dials (marked Rotary 1 through 4) and four buttons that can be mapped (via the programmer) to control parameters of any devices within the Combinator.

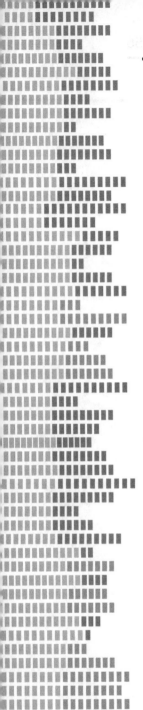

Loading a Pre-Made Combinator

Reason 3.0 comes with a wide selection of pre-made patches for use with the Combinator. Some of these have not only customized sounds and effects but also pre-set patterns so you can hear a mini-song that you can incorporate into your song.

1. Click on the Browse Patch button on the Combinator and browse to Reason Factory Sound Bank > Combinator Patches > Performance Patches > Drum&Bass Live Template [Run].cmb. Double click on it or select it and click OK.

2. On the Combinator face click on the Run Pattern Devices button if it is not already selected. It will light up red and begin playing a drum and bass background pattern.

Using the Combine Command

Reason 3.0 allows you to select a group of devices and combine them instantly so they are part of a Combinator. For this example we'll load a demo song and combine some devices with it.

1. Go to the File menu and select Open.

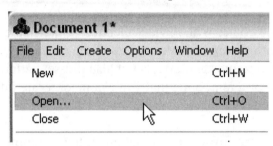

2. Browse to the Reason Folder > Demo Songs > Orkester Demo and double click it or select it and click Open.

3. Scroll down to the bottom of the rack where you'll find a Remix mixer, an RV-7000 and a dozen NN-XT devices.

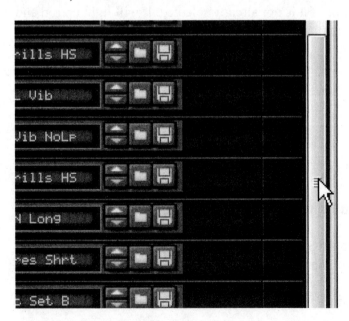

4. Holding down the Shift key, click once on all 14 of these devices. As they become selected, they will each be bound by a small grey outline.

5. Once they are all selected, right click and from the menu select Combine.

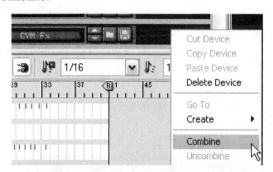

Removing Devices

Do you want to remove some or all of the devices you placed in the Combinator and return them to the rack? Shift click on all the devices you wish to move to the rack, then right click to bring up the menu. Select Uncombine, and the devices will be removed from the Combinator.

All of the devices are now combined and contained within a newly created Combinator. Within the Combinator their routing remains the same.

Dragging and Dropping Devices into the Combinator

You can build up the Combinator by dragging and dropping devices already in the rack into the devices region of the Combinator.

1. Create a 14:2 mixer by right clicking.

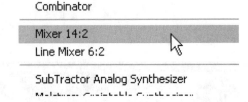

2. Create a SubTractor by right clicking.

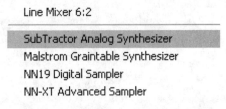

3. Create a Combinator by right clicking.

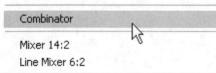

4. If not already selected, click on the Show Devices button so it glows red. A small white-bordered black space will appear beneath the Combinator. There will be a thick red line at the top of this area.

5. Position your pointer on the SubTractor in the handle area (between the screws at the side of the device) and click and hold down your mouse button. Drag it into the device area of the Combinator, then release the mouse button. The SubTractor is now "inside" the Combinator.

Creating Devices with the Combinator

You can build your combination within the Combinator by creating devices just as you would in the rack.

1. Create a 14:2 mixer.

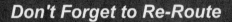

2. Create a Combinator.

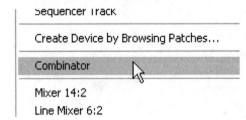

3. If it is not already selected, click on the Show Devices button so it glows red.

4. In the devices region of the Combinator, right click and from the menu select Create > NN-19 Digital Sampler.

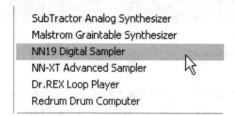

5. Create a UN-16 Unison using the same method.

6. Press Tab to flip the rack around.

The devices in the Combinator are routed together the same way they would be if created that way in the rack. In addition, the final device is routed to the Combinator's "From Devices" port.

Manipulating the Combinator

Just as on the rack, devices within the Combinator can be moved, deleted, routed and re-routed.

Programming the Combinator

The Combinator is one of the most customizable devices in Reason 3.0. Using the programmer, we can map specific device parameters to the different rotary dials and buttons on the Combinator interface.

1. Create a 14:2 Mixer by right clicking.

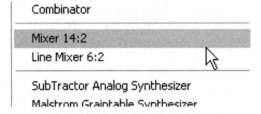

Combinator

Mixer 14:2
Line Mixer 6:2

SubTractor Analog Synthesizer
Malstrom Graintable Synthesizer

2. Create a Combinator by right clicking.

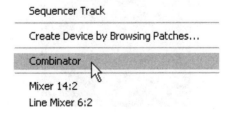

Sequencer Track

Create Device by Browsing Patches...

Combinator

Mixer 14:2
Line Mixer 6:2

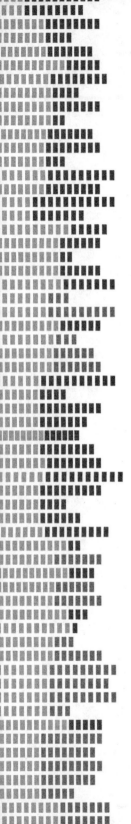

3. Within the Combinator, create a 6:2 Mixer, NN-19 Digital Sampler and SubTractor Analog Synthesizer.

4. Click on the Show Programmer button. It will glow red, and beneath the main interface the Programmer window will be revealed.

5. Along the left side of the programmer, you will see a column called Device with the three devices we created numbered and listed beneath it. Click once where it says Line Mixer. It will be highlighted in light blue.

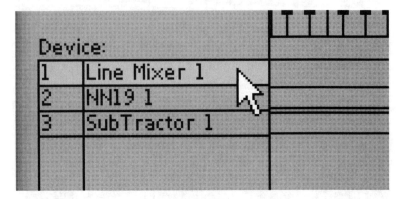

6. On the far right side of the progammer, under Modulation Routing, we will see indicated Device: 1 Line Mixer 1. In the Target column, directly to the right of the column where Rotary 1 is listed, click and hold your mouse button to reveal a menu. Scroll down and select Master Level, then release the mouse button. This will now be listed next to Rotary 1. We have now mapped the master level control of our devices within the Combinator (which are patched into the micro-mix) to the Rotary 1 dial.

7. On the Combinator interface double click on the name Rotary 1 and rename it to Master Level.

We can use this method to program multiple parameters to the different buttons and rotaries on the Combinator interface.

More Programming the Combinator

We can patch parameters from multiple devices to the same dial or button on the Combinator interface.

1. In the key mapping section of the programmer select NN19 1 by clicking on it once so it is highlighted.

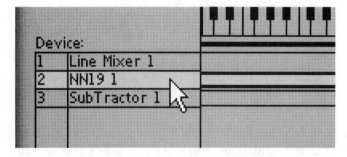

2. In the Target column to the right of Rotary 2 in the modulation routing section, click and hold your mouse button down to reveal the menu and select Pitch Bend.

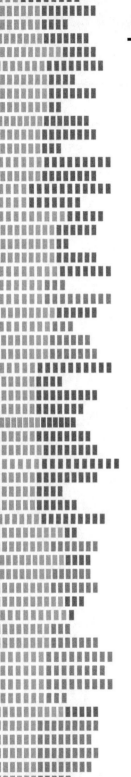

3. In the key mapping section of the programmer select SubTractor 1.

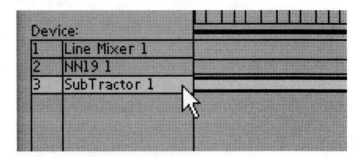

4. Repeat instruction 2.

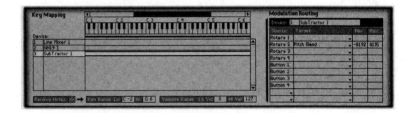

5. Rename Rotary 2 so it is called Pitch Bend.

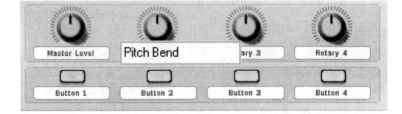

We have now mapped the pitch bend parameters of both the NN19 and the SubTractor to Rotary 2. When you turn this dial, it will bend the pitch on both of these devices at the same time.

More Customization

The Combinator takes you to the next level of customizing by allowing you to choose a backdrop.

1. Right click on the interface and choose Select Backdrop from the menu.

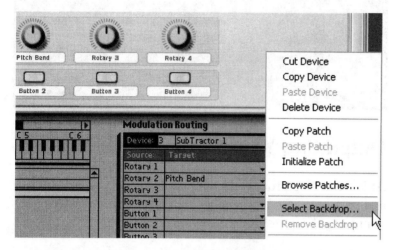

2. Browse to Reason Folder > Template Documents > Combi Backdrops > Template Backdrops.

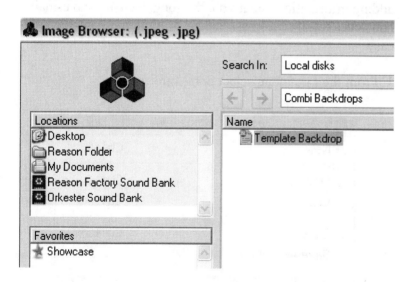

You have now added a new backdrop to your Combinator.

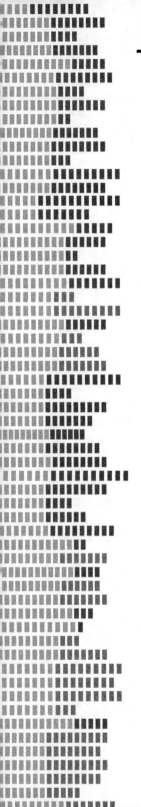

370

Custom Backdrop

Would you like a truly tailored backdrop? Create your own in your favorite graphics program, making sure that the dimensions are 754 x 138 pixels and are a .jpg file.

Outputting Your Song

At last the long process is over. You've poured your heart and creativity into composing, then mixing and mastering your song. Now it's time to share it.

Adding Song Information

Part of putting your stamp on the song you've created is adding information about you, the song, website and e-mail contacts as well as a splash image. Adding these details is easy.

1. From the File menu select Song Information.

File	Edit	Create	Options	Window	Help
New				Ctrl+N	
Open...				Ctrl+O	
Close				Ctrl+W	
Save				Ctrl+S	
Save As...					
Song Information...				Ctrl+I	
Publish Song...					

2. Fill in the fields as desired.

Image Dimensions

Your splash image must be a .bmp (bitmapped) image file 256 x 256.

Publishing Your Song

When you publish your song, it is saved as an .rps or Reason Published Song file. A published song is essentially yours with a number of restrictions applied to it. A published song cannot:

- Be saved.

- Have any of its elements cut, pasted or copied.

- Have any elements exported (if modified).

Publish your song by going to the File menu and selecting Publish Song, then saving your song.

Creating a Self-Contained Song for Collaboration

At times you may wish to move your song including all of its related files to another system or perhaps offer it to a collaborator to work on. When you go to the File menu and select Song Self Contain Settings, a dialog box will open with a list of samples or REX files. You can click on check boxes to select files you wish to include in the self-contained song. Songs with a lock icon next to them are associated with a ReFill and cannot be saved with the song file.

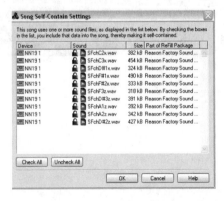

> ## File Size
>
> *Since these self-contained songs include other audio files, they will be much larger than regular song files.*

Exporting the Song as a MIDI or Audio File

For others to be able to listen to your song, you'll need to export it as an audio or MIDI file. The process is quick and easy.

- **Exporting an Audio File** - From the File menu select Export Song as an audio file. Name the file, then save it as a Windows WAVE file (.wav) or Audio IFF file (.aif).

- **Exporting a MIDI File** - From the File menu select Export Song as a MIDI file. Name the file, then save it as a standard MIDI file (.mid).

Index

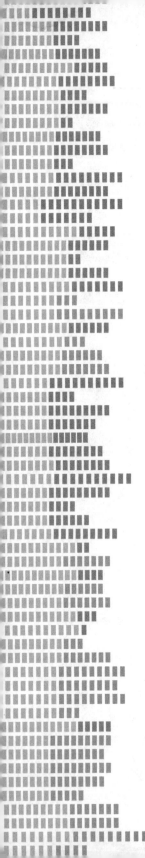

Also Available From Mimosa Books:

eBay SCAMS!
PROTECT YOURSELF AS YOU MASTER eBay
MARK GABRIEL